# THE
# NO FAD
# GOOD FOOD
# $5 A WEEK
# COOKBOOK

# THE
# NO FAD
# GOOD FOOD
# $5 A WEEK
# COOKBOOK

Caroline Ackerman

Dodd, Mead & Company
*New York*

ISBN: 0-396-07071-X

Published simultaneously in Canada
by McClelland and Stewart Limited

Dodd, Mead & Company
New York

Dedicated to Jerry Ackerman for saying, "Yes, do it."

Thanks to Dr. Elizabeth Smith and the University of Manitoba for taking me on as a special project student, and to Tom and Barbara Carney for reading the manuscript and making valuable suggestions.

If your son asks for a fish
Will you give him a serpent?
If he asks for bread
Will you give him a stone?
J. C.

If he asks for food
Will you give him
   Jell-o
      Cake
         Coke
            Sugar Pops
               Potato Chips
                  Strawberry Shoelaces?

# Contents

# List of Tables

# INTRODUCTION

One year we hiked the Rocky Mountains near Banff and Jasper in Alberta. I, the senior citizen of the group; Eddy, my son, the teeny bopper. We came out to the highway finally exhausted by rain and snow and wrong turns, hoping to catch a ride into Jasper. The vehicles whizzed by us – cars, large cars, vans, trucks, campers, cars pulling trailers, huge family buses and all carrying canoes and boats and motors and bicycles and motor cycles. How curious, the things people bring when coming to meet the mountains. In Jasper, one of our group went to visit some friends, leaving the rest of us in camp. That evening we were relaxing after a meal of chili con frijoles, corn pone, and bean sprouts, when he returned.

"Guess what I've just eaten? Roast beef, yorkshire pudding, mashed potatoes, gravy, chocolate cake." Nobody moved.

"Yeah?...that's what I thought you'd say. I wasn't very impressed either."

It dawned on us that we'd been eating a near vegetarian diet for two weeks while engaging in enormous activity. We'd loved every meal of it. We felt not one whit worse for the experience and we weren't even anxious to get back to normal.

Bouncing along home on the Greyhound bus, I puzzled over my experiences. How many years had I been studying nutrition and feeding a family only to find now out that meat is not necessary to health and well-being? I had always known it somewhere in my mind as a theory. What an idea that perhaps many of the food mores and practices which I had always assumed to be ordained by God may be no more a necessity to good nutrition than the camper-trailer-motorbike-boat assembly is to seeing the Rockies. In those moments I decided to write a book to share my new found knowledge that beans can be beautiful; that we can live a little closer to life by simplifying our eating habits.

Back in Winnipeg I enrolled in the University of Manitoba, a special student with a special project, *The Investigation of a Low Cost Alternative to the Typical North American Dietary*, under the direction of Dr. Elizabeth Smith and spent the winter checking into the nutritional implications of North Americans eating a meat-free diet. I searched out recipes that would be delicious, nutritious and cheap, and hired some help to test them. We planned and carried out a two week test diet weighing every bit of food eaten by five people, put the amounts of each through the Nutrition Department computer program for nutrient checks. We carefully priced amounts of foods used in local supermarkets and grocery stores.

This book is an attempt to share with you some of our findings.

# PART ONE

## Food Habits and Attitudes
## of
## North Americans

# The North American Diet:
## Whats Wrong With It?

### Breakfast

Orange Juice
Bacon & Eggs
Toast & Jam
Coffee
Milk

### Lunch

Soup
Sandwiches
Fruit or Cookie
Coffee/Tea/Milk

### Dinner

Meat entrée
Potato
Vegetable
or Salad
Dessert
Coffee/Tea/Milk

This specimen menu or slight variations of it is consumed by millions of North Americans 365 days a year. Some people eat cereal for breakfast in addition to eggs or instead of eggs. Some people skip breakfast. Some people skip lunch. Beans or macaroni and cheese are sometimes substituted for meat at dinner. Some people don't eat potatoes. Some people don't eat salads. But for the purposes of this book we will call the above the "North American diet."

I really hate to knock this typical North American dietary. I like every item on the specimen menu. It is nourishing and can be very tasty. I grew up on this diet as did millions of Canadians and Americans. But in all honesty, I have to say there are some things wrong with it when evaluated in any context other than nutrition class, Family Circle Magazine, Safeway colour posters and TV Jello ads.

The typical North American diet is:

Too expensive.
Too complicated.
Too standardized.
Considered an absolute.
Too much.
Making inefficient use of the earth's resources.
Too refined.
Too different from the diets of the rest of the world.
Putting us out on a limb.

## Too Expensive

How much did you spend at the supermarket last week? At the corner grocery store? How much for lunches? Snacks? Candy bars or soft drinks? Chances are you spent far more than you wanted to. Inflation keeps driving all prices up. In recent years food prices have climbed more than the general price index. If your income has climbed at the same rate or better, you have no real worry, but many incomes have remained the same or become less.

Study the chart on page 129. The figures show that thirty-four percent of our calories come from meat, eggs, and dairy products (excluding butter.) These foods are basically expensive by any measure. There is no way to make meat cheap. It requires large inputs of scarce resources:

Water
Land
High Protein Feed
Labour
Management (at every level of production)
Government Regulation
Processing
Transportation
Cold Storage

We depend heavily on these foods for our nutrients. (Note that we get 69% of our protein from these foods.) We are getting something of great value to us for our money. Thirty-four percent of our calories come from fats and sugars which contain almost no nutrients except for calories. Twenty percent of our calories come from cereals which sometimes do and sometimes don't contain important nutrients. These two classes of foods which make up fifty percent of our calories are basically cheap but are made expensive by the refinement and processing we demand in them. We don't eat demerara sugar, straight run whole wheat flour, brown rice and simple vegetable oil. We drink Coke and eat white sugar and candy bars. We eat white bread and danish pastries, rice krispies and potato chips. Changing cheap sugars, fats, cereals into the dainties we desire costs us dearly in terms of technology, equipment, management, labour and attempted disposal of resultant pollution. In a world of energy shortage, technology shortage, management shortage and daily worsening pollution, perhaps we should ask ourselves if we don't want to take our foods in a less expensive form.

Food prices in relation to a standard value dollar should have come down markedly in this century. Increased land and labour productivity, high yield crops, high food conversion of livestock should mean low food prices for the consumer. However, much of the price lowering effects of technical advances are offset by increased costs of ultra refinement, subsequent enrichment, product differentiation, advertising and other ploys to con the consumer, research into how to create illusions – how to get more air and water into consumer products, and industry expenses such as yachts, plush carpets, and government lobbying. We have to pay for all this when we buy *Jell-O, Hostess Cup-Cakes* or *Minute Rice*.

It is an interesting game as you go through a supermarket to think of the foods on display in terms of what they are basically, and to compare prices with a less glamorous form of the same food. Corn flakes are basically cornmeal (less valuable nutritionally, but made from cornmeal.) Price in March, 1974: cornflakes, 57¢/lb; cornmeal, 38¢/lb. Potato chips are roughly half potato, half fat. If potatoes are 13¢/lb. and oil is 40¢/lb., then 1 lb. of a 50:50 mix would be 28¢. Potato chips

14

are $1.06/lb. How much turkey and how much flour are contained in a tin of turkey noodle soup? We pay a lot for our food.

In comparison to what most of the people of the world pay for food we spend a fortune. In comparison to what we need to spend to nourish ourselves, we spend a fortune.

When you know you can feed yourself for $200-$400/year or your family of five for $1,000-$2,000/year, you may look at your $5,000 or $15,000 paycheck in a different light. You may start looking at yourself as rich instead of poor. Really you are rich, you know, compared to any global or historical standard.

## Too Complicated

Eating in North America is far too complicated. The array of foods required is time consuming and tedious to shop for, bulky and heavy to transport, expensive to store, requires a considerable amount of labour and extensive equipment to make ready for consumption. Not only must we pay large amounts of money for our typical North American diet, we have to spend one to two hours pe·week choosing this food. We need a car, if not a station wagon to haul it home. We need 200 square feet of cupboard space to store it. We spend anywhere from 1 to 4 hours in the kitchen per day further processing it. We require a four burner stove and an oven, a 14 cubic foot refrigerator and a 21 cubic foot freezer, an electric kettle (if you're Canadian,) a special machine for making toast, for making coffee, an electric frying pan, a mixing machine, a blending machine, an ice crushing machine, a can opening machine, and an electric knife to make the eight bags of highly processed food table-ready. We throw away a lot of it so we have to buy a special garbage grinding machine to pulverize the leftovers so that they can be easily dumped into the polluted river.

## Too Standardized

The typical North American diet is too standardized. The orange juice is standardized, the bacon is standardized, the cake is standardized, the bread for toast is standardized, the jam for the toast is standardized, the soup is standardized, and on it goes. Standardization is a phenomenon we should know about and think about carefully because given big business, big government, and our present economic attitudes, we will be experiencing more standardization and at an increasing rate. It is a mixed blessing.

As people cook less and buy more ready-to-eat products, and as restaurants cook less and buy more prepared and semi-prepared foods, cooking technology becomes the province of the big company. Gone is the pressure for young girls and young men to learn to cook. Gone is the skill of cooking in the family and in the community. Gone is the experience of cooking with its challenge and reward. Gone is the sense of worth and independence of the person who is able to look after his own ordinary needs. When the day comes that there are no cooks – when mothers know only how to "follow the simple directions on the package" we will be sorry.

One result of this is that salesmanship is being substituted for real satisfaction. As I chewed the peanut butter between slices of pasty bread one day I gazed resentfully at the bread wrapper. *Hill Billy Bread*, it said, and it showed a picture of a long man sitting against a tree, legs stretched across green grass. The bread was identical to other soft, pasty, unpalatable bread I had eaten many times. Why was it called *Hill Billy Bread*? The bakery was capitalizing on the fact that people remember with satisfaction eating good bread in the "hills" or else have heard rumours of such. It was selling the *suggestion* of satisfaction, rather than a satisfying product.


**Considered an Absolute**

The typical *North American Diet* is considered an absolute. What starts out being the prize, sought after by everyone and awarded to the successful, may end up being a millstone. Chicken *every* Sunday may be a privilege and a special blessing, or it may be a sentence.

We come from a long line´of kings, movie queens, police chiefs, preachers, school teachers, fathers and mothers; and we have been obedient subjects, admirers, private citizens, congregations, pupils and children. When a suitable authority holds up a chart showing the typical *North American Diet* and tells us it is good for us and that we, our children and our children's children should eat these foods every day, we dutifully do our best to comply. Those who aren't able to eat the prescription, imitate it as closely as possible and keep trying. Those who choose not to follow it sustain guilt feelings about their aberrant behaviour.

The authorities who have issued the edicts regarding our food patterns are the general culture and the nutritionists and government agencies. The culture has given us the porridge, eggs, toast, soup, meat, potato and pie picture. The nutrition profession issued models for us to follow.

The government agencies and other public institutions spread this word to captive audiences. Food companies pick it up making it palatable and profitable and sell it, or a reasonable looking facsimile, to everybody. (Kraft pushing cheese, General Mills pushing breakfast cereal, Florida citrus growers pushing oranges, Swift pushing meat.)

Trying to follow an absolute always gives problems. You are resistant to new information. You miss a lot of ideas for good and very enjoyable food. How long did we daringly eat Chop Suey, a good old British stew with boiled bean sprouts and a bit of soy sauce, before we discovered some of the truly wonderful things that Chinese people really eat.

Then when you become disenchanted, you may abandon the old absolute. But you don't feel comfortable so you search until you find a new absolute to take its place. The new one may be worse. It may be more limiting and just as inefficient in terms of filling your real needs.

Two basic facts of life have greatly favoured survival of mankind on earth. One is that the nutrients required by man for life and growth are widely distributed in thousands of edible plants and animals. The second is that human digestion is able to make use of most of them. Are you tired of paying homage to an absolute? Perhaps it is time for you to get acquainted with some of the other good things around you.

You might become interested in nutrition. You might read some books on the subject, talk to professionals and friends and look to your own experience. There's lots to find out.

## Too Much

The pioneers starved their first winters in the New World. Friendly Indians taught them how to use the bountiful resources of the land, solving the problem of starvation in what would become the USA and Canada. The settlers then separated the Indians from their land, drove them off, killed them when they refused to go, thus securing for themselves and their posterity, 3 million square miles of untapped natural resources; land, water, timber, game, minerals – unprecedented wealth – and the freedom and drive to exploit it.

The custom of plenty is as much a part of my being as the love of sunshine or the feel of warm sand under my feet. I like to say to the friend or stranger at my door, "Come on in; stay for dinner; we have plenty." I love a feast, twenty brimming dishes of tempting goodness – eager feasters, plates in hand, salivary glands awash, waiting for the blessing to be said. The joyous comraderie of communal gluttony is extremely pleasing to my senses. Now and then, however, I detect a cause to pause, to view the picture more closely and in wider perspective. I see the greater part of 250 million North Americans feasting; not four times a year, not once a month or every Sunday, but three times every day. I see an obese housewife spending one hour making an apple pie, to serve to a tired, overweight husband and two indifferent children. The pie is prepared and served in memory of the past, a feeble pathetic attempt to bring back the feeling of a day when Grandmother made six apple pies to feed a hungry family and ten threshing hands who had expended huge amounts of energy doing meaningful tasks of grand physical challenge. Alas, the ploy doesn't work. Half the pie is thrown out or it is eaten and carried around under bulging belts until someone screams "diet!"

Our population carries around too much adipose tissue . . . fat. Old people are overweight, teenagers are overweight, even babies are overweight. Let's begin by saying that it is beneficial to have some fat on your body. Bits of fat here and there are a vital part of your body structure. Some is useful around your abdominal organs for cushioning. More is needed to meet an unforeseen period of famine or a bout of flu. But what about the millions of pounds of excess weight that North Americans carry around daily? What's wrong with it? First, it is extra work. Suppose you are a female of average build, five feet four inches tall. Your ideal weight is 125. If you weigh 137, you are 10% overweight. That doesn't sound very impressive. Just for fun try carrying 12 pounds of flour around with you for three days.

For extra weight, your body must build extra muscle, extra blood vessels, extra skin. Your heart has to work more and you have to eat more to accommodate the excess weight. It is worth the extra metabolic work if next week or next month the fat is going to save you from starvation. Otherwise it is a burden.

My friend, who has used crutches for several years because of a congenital hip condition, would be less dependent on them if she would get rid of 35 pounds of fat. My neighbour who is crippled with arthritis in her knee joints could walk much better if she would lose 50 pounds. We bear a lot of unnecessary burdens.

## Makes Inefficient Use of the World's Resources

North American eating habits are extremely wasteful. You know about the greedy garburator, the plate waste and refrigerator ruin in your own kitchen. Not only is this waste a strain on scarce food supplies in a hungry world, but its decomposition is also a burden on our ecosystem.

But even the food we eat represents inefficient use of the world's resources. According to the Canadian Dietary Standard (chart, page 131) an adult ma!e weighing 158 pounds consuming a diet as outlined in Canada's Food Guide needs 48 grams of protein each day. According to the *Food and Agriculture Organization* of the U.N. (FAO) Food Balance Sheets for 1957-59, Canadians consume 95 grams of protein each day. The excess of protein we eat over what we need is deaminated* by the liver and excreted as urea and of course goes on to further polute the poor old river.

Seventy percent of the protein of North Americans comes from animal sources – meat, eggs, dairy products. Protein in the form of animal flesh is the most expensive kind for the world to produce. Seven pounds of grain fed to a steer produce about one pound of beef. Eggs and milk are somewhat more efficiently produced, but are still very dear.

Aaron Altschul in his very readable and informative book, *Proteins, Their Chemistry and Politics*, explains protein cost using some picturesque comparisons.

If a person needs 1,000,000 calories in a year, 3½ acres of land would be needed to produce enough meat and milk to

---

* deaminated – split up – the nitrogen portion is disposed of by the kidneys, the plumbing, the river. The rest of the molecule is used for energy the same as in carbohydrates.

feed him; one quarter acre would produce enough wheat to feed him; 1/7 acre (in Japan) would produce enough rice and beans.

Seven plant calories are required to produce one animal calorie.

## The Cost to the World of Two Different Dietaries

**a In terms of plant calories:**

|  | Calories per day | % Calories from Animal Sources | Plant Calories required to produce this diet |
|---|---|---|---|
| Country #1 | 2,025 | 10 | 3,240 |
| Country #2 | 3,140 | 35 | 9,734 |

Looking at the caloric consumption of the two countries you deduce that the rich country consumes 50% more than the poor country. But figured in terms of plant calories required to produce each diet, the rich country consumes three times as much.

**b In terms of water:**

|  | Daily Food Consumption Per capita | Amount of Water Required to produce it |
|---|---|---|
| Country #1 | 2½ lbs. bread | 300 gallons |
| Country #2 | 2 lbs. bread & 1 lb. meat | 2,500 gallons |

Consider the ounce of crispy bacon you ate for breakfast. It took 3.6 ounces of raw bacon to make it. You threw away the fat in the pan and that absorbed by the paper towel. Someone had to feed 1.3 pounds of grain to a pig to make the 3.6 ounces of bacon. (That's using 3.6:1 feed conversion and 60% carcass yield.) The grain mix was about 12% protein. Your bacon was about 30% protein. For your .3 ounces of protein, the world had to pay 2.5 ounces. In fact, if you had eaten the 1.3 pounds of grain you would have gotten something like 1900 calories, (more than the daily caloric requirement for lots of adults,) enough protein for many adults for a day, as well as generous amounts of iron and B vitamins. This is the cost to the world of your few bites of

20

crispy bacon. I'm not knocking bacon, but please be aware when you eat it that you are eating very expensive food.

We now understand better that the earth's resources are not boundless and endless. It is time to become considerate in the demands we make on the earth. We must discover how to make wise use of the bounty of life at our feet and in our hands.

## Too Refined

The typical diet of North Americans is too far removed from the natural earthy sources of things. We demand refinement in our food because we have come to associate refinement of grain and sugar and oil with refinement of person.

A million years of genetic wisdom is built into a kernel of wheat. In 75 years of nutrition research into nutrient requirements of human beings we think we know all there is to know about eating wheat. When human vanity demands white bread, we confidently remove the most nutritious parts of the wheat and doctor the finished product with an iron compound and some B vitamins, bleach, dough conditioners, etc. In converting the flour into consumer items refined oil and white sugar and flavourings are added. It seems incredible that we would do such a thing to ourselves. But through advertising and cake baking contests, we are hooked. We think we must have sweet, fat dainties and refined, white bread for our happiness. Even adding meat and milk to the refined oil, sugar and flour does not solve the problem completely. Our bodies were designed slowly through evolution along with the wheat kernel and bean. Our digestions were developed to handle meat and grains and vegetables. Roughage, at least, is lacking in a highly refined diet. What else is lacking?

## What's Wrong with Cap'n Crunch (And Sugar Pops and Honey Comb Cereal and Count Chocula)

1. It's too soft, it provides no exercise for the teeth and gums.
2. It's too sweet; it provides lots of sugar to encourage cariogenic bacteria.

3. It isn't satisfying. For the first time in a few years, I tried a handful of Cap'n Crunch. I tossed a few puffs into my mouth thinking, "It's probably much better than I remember. How could nice little brown balls be that bad? . . . Crunch, Phoney! It is worse than I remembered." It just doesn't taste good.

### NUTRIENT CONTENT OF ONE OUNCE OF TWO BREAKFAST CEREALS

|  | Cal | Pro | Ca | Fe | A | Thi | Rib | Nia |
|---|---|---|---|---|---|---|---|---|
| Granola (Recipe page ) | 150 | 3.7 | 19 | 1.2 | 150 | 1.76 | .06 | .04 |
| Puffed presweetened corn cereal | 130 | 1.0 | 3 | .5 | - | .12 | .05 | .6 |

SOURCE: USDA HANDBOOK NO. 8.

Actually, there was more difference in the home made granola and the Cap'n Crunch than I expected. Granola provides very respectable amounts of protein, iron, thiamin and niacin which is what we expect from whole grain, what we tradionally get from a good cereal while Cap'n Crunch has nothing to brag about except niacin.

## Too Different From The Diets Of The Rest Of The World

It is in poor taste for me to feast and waste while my brother in the next room dies of starvation. Modern science, if not social science and the individual conscience, has made it obvious that all men are brothers. Our interdependence is inescapable. We sink or swim as a species.

We have come to accept vast discrepancies in standards of consumption (for comparison of protein and calorie consumption in different countries see the table on page 20) as normal and unchangeable. "If I starve myself, it won't necessarily increase the food supply of an African family. Who will profit if I reduce my consumption and energy level to the world average? What about distribution?" One moment, please. You are not concerned about distribution. You are trying to change the subject. So long as we are uniformly bound by our habits and cultural practices, so long as we are operating out of fear, we are unable to consider the problem of hunger on a world basis. The points we bring up are irrelevant attention getters put forth to ensure that no solution will be found. Although I am not personally responsible for the low wages paid to the worker on a banana plantation by United Fruit Company for example, the very fact that I can buy bananas more cheaply that I can buy B.C. apples, shows that I indirectly benefit from their misery.

I am terribly afraid inside that a solution to the problem of poverty of which hunger is a part, will include decreasing my own consumption. This strikes terror to my heart because I look to possession of consumption goods for my sense of security. I dare not think what will happen if I have less.

As I reviewed professional opinion and research projects aimed at establishing minimum human amino acid requirements, I became aware of an attitude that grated my nerves. For a long time I couldn't articulate my objection until I read a report of W. C. Rose on his ten-year study of amino acids in human metabolism. Dr. Rose was saying that for the test he developed the practice of using two times the highest observed minimum requirement of a given amino acid in establishing the minimum requirements for another amino acid. A little later he explains " . . . discretion dictates that any error be in the direction of liberality." This has been part of an overall attitude toward nutrition which is a greedy, haughty attitude on a world basis. We cannot continue as individuals or as a country to insulate ourselves, in face of limited world supplies of resources, by this theory, let any error be in the direction of liberality . . . for us. I am led to the image of myself and my country as a blind pig slopping away in a full trough, limited in his life experience and potential by his blindness and his obesity. Outside the fence stand gazing the other barnyard animals starving and tired of starving. Will they conclude, "Let us separate this blind, fat pig from his wealth. It will be a kindness to him and to us?"

Gluttony in the face of deprivation is provocative and decidedly unfriendly. It is also limiting of the glutton because to continue in his gluttony, he must guard against the reception of information about the rest of the world lest his heart be touched and he be tempted to share his hoard.

**Puts Us Out on a Limb**
Our diet of very nourishing, very expensive food, plus high

calorie super refined food puts us in a bit of an awkward position. 33% of our food comes from animal sources: nutritionally concentrated – very expensive – also very perishable. 33% of our food is refined fats and sugars supplying almost nothing for our bodies except fuel value. They lend themselves to seasoning, flavouring, colouring, crisping and have long shelf life. Fruits and vegetables, comparatively expensive and largely perishable furnish about one tenth of our food energy. Cereal grains form about 20% of our diets. These are potentially very inexpensive sources of nutritionally valuable food. The nutrients are depleted and the cost is increased by the refinement we demand. Some minerals and synthetic vitamins are added to much of the refined product at additional expense.

In a way this is a good dietary. It gives most of us the nutrients we need. In another way it puts us out on a limb nutritionally. What would happen if we had a national emergency? For instance, if the electric power went off, without refrigeration the meat and dairy products we depend on for so much of our nourishment would begin to rot. In ten days they would be very scarce. We would be left with white flour, white sugar, and purified fat. We would starve. We are quite dependent on the smooth running of our very specialized processing and distribution systems. We lack the customs, the raw materials and the technology for a satisfactory alternative.

Even small scale emergencies point to a basic weakness of our consumption pattern. Consider for instance that father doesn't bring home a paycheck and all of a sudden there is half the usual $60.00 to buy groceries for a week. Instead of buying roast beef, chicken, pork chops, the mother will buy Kraft dinner, bologna, "pork and beans." She will serve these dishes in place of the meat she can't afford. The rest of the family's diet will remain the same. The kids will eat just as much candy, cookies, soft drinks, potato chips, white bread and jam. They may even eat more of the junk food because they don't like the substitute dinners as well as the usual ones and eat less of them.

Suppose the mother is sick or out working or doing something else and doesn't put meals on the table. The children feed themselves. They help themselves to whatever is easy and familiar: Sugar Pops and milk, canned soup, hot dogs, bread and peanut butter, candy bars, soft drinks, etc.

24

Or try this. Go downtown at meal time with 35¢ in your pocket – no more. When you get hungry, begin to look for something to eat. What can you buy? Candy . . . yes. Soft drink? . . . yes. Potato chips? . . . yes. A sweet roll? . . . probably. Ice cream? . . . probably. None of these would provide you with appreciably more than calories. How many children, teenagers, old people, poor people are downtown with only 35¢ in their pockets? Our traditions assume that:

A  no one will have as little as 35¢ when downtown at mealtime or

B  that it will happen rarely, and that the person will soon have a hearty meal back home, or

C  that a candy bar and a coke are nourishing food, or

D  that it doesn't matter whether people are well fed or not.

None of us like the picture of starving or half starved people in our midst. We all know that candy bars and Cokes are not nourishing food. Maybe we haven't realized that a candy bar and a coke are very filling to a little girl. Having eaten it she won't likely eat a hearty meal even if offered one. Maybe we haven't noticed how many meals are not eaten at home. Tons of calorie rich, nutrient poor foods are eaten daily by children, teenagers, old people, poor people *instead* of meals. Some of these people ate very little breakfast and will find a *sparse* supper when they get home.

These small emergencies represent everyday life to many people in our very affluent country. We sorely need to discover ways to build satisfying nutritionally adequate low cost diets.

**Suggestion Of An Alternative**

What can you do? For those interested in change I would recommend:

1.  Get out of the competition for scarce or highly valued resources such as beef and pork and chicken and ready made pizza, canned mushroom soup, and expensive off season delicacies. I am not saying, "Don't eat pork and don't eat oranges." I am not knocking the raising of pigs or the growing of oranges. I'm not knocking trade.

I'm knocking the lock-step parade of miserable competition and conformity and fear. I'm knocking:

> Gimme my pork
> Gimme my beef
> Gimme my orange juice
> Hamburger is $1.50 a pound and they can't do that to us.
> We haven't had steak for 6 months and *they can't-do-that-to-us!*
> Studies have shown that people in Carman, Manitoba have a . . . juice deficiency!

**2.** Relax and be your body. Be united with your sense of taste and smell. Be friendly with your digestion. Perhaps you can know better when to eat, what is edible, when to stop eating. Your teeth are strong. Chew with them. Be aware of taste and chewing. As you do this for a few days, you will be amazed.

**3.** Get acquainted with new foods. Make a study of nutrition so that you may determine how to fill your nutritional needs from sources available to you and so that you can learn how to spot a deficiency in a given array of foods.

**4.** Quit playing the supermarket game with its bargains and prizes and spiralling prices. Consider whether you really want to be a part of the refinement-enrichment routine.

**5.** Become more self reliant. Would you like to learn to cook? To make bread, soup, yogurt, cheese? It is easy to learn.

**6.** Form a co-op to study food resources and to purchase the food you want.

**7.** For the description of a food plan designed for the "Intelligent Pauper," please turn the page.

# PART TWO

## The Weekly Food List

## Your Key to Adequate
## Nutrition at Rock Bottom Prices

I am about to tell you how to feed yourself . . . CHEAPLY!
It will be so easy that you won't believe it. Your diet will be
based on the following foods:

> Whole grains
> Legumes
> Skimmed milk powder
> Eggs
> Cabbage
> Rutabaga turnips
> Potatoes
> Fortified margarine and other fats
> Sugars, salt, spices, flavourings, fruit
> Other things just for fun

### Why Choose This Combination of Foods?

Because they are nutritious. In the amounts shown in the
Weekly Food List (page 32), they will supply you with more
than the Canadian Dietary Standard for essential nutrients.

Because they are cheap and available almost everywhere.

Because they are tasty and versatile. These foods have
been used for centuries and recipes for their use can easily be
found. These foods adapt themselves readily to your own
creative endeavours.

Because most of them can be bought in bulk a few times a
year, reducing the burden and confusion of the weekly shop-
ping trip.

Because they require only simple, inexpensive storage.

## The Weekly Food List

This buying guide was developed after library inquiry into the nutrient needs of humans, the nutrient content of foods and a two week feeding experiment testing palatability and nutritional adequacy.* The exact amount of food you need for a given day or a given week depends on your weight, your body make-up (the proportion of fat to lean body tissue), your basic metabolism rate, (the rate at which you use up energy when you are resting), and the amount of energy you need for your daily activities. Nobody can tell you exactly how much food you need for a given day because things inside your body are always changing and things in your external environment are always changing. This is something only your appetite and/or the bathroom scales can tell you. Most people use up calories at the rate of 15 to 25 calories per pound of body weight per day. The weekly Food List is based on the assumption that your needs fall in the middle of that range, that you will need approximately 20 calories per pound of your own weight per day. If you run out of food and you are still hungry or you start losing weight, you will know that you need more food. If you have food left over and remain the same weight or if you begin to gain weight, you'll know that you have allotted too many calories. If you lose weight and have food left over, you'll know you are an awful cook and need a few lessons.

## How to Use the Weekly Food List

As in the sample family, (page 32) first record your weight or the weight of the group at the top of the page. Record the number of children and the number of adults. Record the amount of your weekly food budget. (*You* may be aiming at $5 per week.) Notice that the amounts of food listed under the heading *Amounts Required* are either per child, per adult, per person, or per 100 pounds of person/weight. Take this literally. Multiply the per child, per adult, per person

---

* Results of the test diet showed that intakes of each nutrient calculated were substantially higher than the Canadian Dietary Standard for the group. Morale among the subjects was high. Complaints were few and mostly related to the problem of eating differently than friends and colleagues.

For detailed nutrient intakes see appendix page 132.

amounts by the number of children, adults, and persons in your group. Multiply the per 100 lb. amounts by the % of 100 pounds represented by you or your group. For the "fat" item, subtract the amounts of butter or margarine needed from the amount "total fat" needed. The remainder is the amount of other fats you require.

Suppose the group, your family, is composed of 3 children and 2 adults with a combined weight of 450 pounds. Multiply the amount of grains required, 4 lbs. per 100 lbs., by 4.5. Write down 18 lb. under the *amount to buy* heading opposite grains. Multiply the amount of legumes required, .5 lb/100 lb., by 4.5 and write down 2.2. lb. The amount of skimmed milk powder is indicated in two ways: .7 lb/100 lb. and .7 lb/child. First multiply .7 lb. by 4.5 and write down 3.2. Then multiply .7 lb. by 3 and write down 2.1. Add the two for a total of 5.3, the amount of skimmed milk powder needed. The eggs are listed as 7 medium/person. Multiply this by 5 and write down 35 eggs. Do the same for the vegetables and write down 3 lb. of each except 5 lb. for potatoes.

---

## MEAN DAILY NUTRIENT INTAKES FOR TEST FAMILY
## ON THE TWO WEEK TEST DIET

### (compared to the Canadian Dietary Standard for that group)

|  | Calculated Intakes | Dietary Standard |  |
|---|---|---|---|
| Calories | 9400 | 12,500 | −25% |
| Protein gm. | 300 | 176[1] | +70% |
| Calcium mg. | 5200 | 4,400 | +18% |
| Iron mg. | 58 | 45 | +28% |
| Vitamin A I U | 33250 | 13,250 | +150%[2] |
| Thiamin mg. | 6.9 | 3.9 | +77% |
| Riboflavin mg. | 8.1 | 6.2 | +31% |
| Niacin mg. | 54 | 39 | +37% |
| Vitamin C mg. | 370 | 150 | +148% |

[1] The adjusted figure (using a protein score of 58 for the test diet instead of 70 as used for the typical Canadian diet), would be 50%.

[2] The adjusted figure (supposing ½ value for the vegetable based Vitamin A) would be 20,000 IU/day or 51% above CDS.

31

For fats, multiply the total fats, .8/100 lb. by 4.5 and write down 3.6. Multiply the .3 lb. margarine per child by 3 and write down .9 lb. Add the .5 lb/adult by 2 and write down 1. Add the /child and the /adult margarine and write down 1.9 for total butter or margarine. Subtract this from the figure for total fats, 3.6 and write down 1.7 lb. of other fats. Multiply the .8 lb. sugar by 4.5 and write down 3.6. List the approximate price per pound you expect to pay for each item and multiply that figure by the number of pounds you need

---

### WEEKLY FOOD LIST

Name of person or group    The Sample Family    Date    1974

Number of Adults   2     Number of Children    3

Weight of person or group 450 lbs.   Weekly Food Budget $21.00

| Food | Amounts Required | Amounts To Buy lb | Price Per lb | Cost |
|---|---|---|---|---|
| Grains | 4.0 lb/100 lb | 18.0 | * | 5.66 |
| Legumes | .5 lb/100 lb | 2.2 | * | 1.37 |
| Skim Milk Powder | .7 lb/100 lb | 3.2 | | |
| | plus .7 lb/child | 2.1 | | |
| | Total SMP | 5.3 | .60 | 3.18 |
| Eggs | 7 Medium | 35 eggs | .07 | 2.45 |
| Vegetables | /person | | | |
|   Cabbage | .6 lb/person | 3.0 | .12 | .36 |
|   Carrots | .6 lb/person | 3.0 | .13 | .39 |
|   Potatoes | 1.0 lb/person | 5.0 | .08 | .40 |
|   Rutabagas | .6 lb/person | 3.0 | .12 | .36 |
| Fats | | | | |
|   Total fats | .8 lb/100 lb | 3.6 | | |
|   Butter or | | | | |
|    fortified margarine | .3 lb/child | .9 | | |
| | .5 lb/adult | 1.0 | | |
| Total butter or margarine | | 1.9 | .39 | .74 |
| Other fats | | 1.7 | * | .52 |
| Sugars | .8 lb/100 lb | 3.6 | * | 1.54 |
| Total Cost for Basics | | | | 16.81 |
| Weekly Food Budget | | | | 21.00 |
| Miscellaneous | | | | 4.03 |

*See detail sheet

to buy. Write down the result under *Cost*. For a more accurate picture, see the Detail Sheet, below. Total these costs and subtract this figure from the amount of your weekly food budget. This will give you the amount you have left to spend on miscellaneous food items. If the cost total is higher than your weekly food budget, you have to find cheaper sources of supply or increase your food budget.

This diet is set up so that (following the Restraints, below) when you fill your caloric requirements, your other nutrients

## DETAIL SHEET

| Name | Sample Family | | |
|---|---|---|---|
| Specific Food | Amount | Price | Cost* |
| Food Category | to buy | Per lb. | |
| **Grains** | lb | $ | $ |
| Whole Wheat Flour | 6 | .17 | 1.02 |
| Rolled Oats | 4 | .23 | .92 |
| Brown Rice | 2 | .55 | 1.10 |
| Dark Rye Flour | 1.5 | .17 | .26 |
| Whole Barley | 1.0 | .23 | .23 |
| Millet | .5 | .50 | .25 |
| Peanuts | 1.0 | .88 | .88 |
| Miscellaneous nuts and grains | 2.0 | .50 | 1.00 |
| | 18.0 | | 5.66 |
| | .5 | | |
| | 17.5 | | |
| **Legumes** | | | |
| (grains .5 lb short. Add .5 lb to legumes) | | | |
| Split Peas | .7 | .39 | .27 |
| Soy Beans | .5 | .59 | .30 |
| Beans | 1.5 | .53 | .80 |
| | 2.7 | | 1.37 |
| **Other Fats** | | | |
| Vegetable Oil | 1.2 | .40 | .52 |
| Fat from Peanuts | .5 | above | |
| **Sugars** | | | |
| Honey | .5 | .85 | .43 |
| Molasses | 1.0 | .28 | .28 |
| Brown Sugar | .6 | .33 | .20 |
| Raisins | .5 | .66 | .33 |
| Dates | 1.0 | .30 | .30 |
| | 3.6 | | 1.54 |

\* Prices taken at a Winnipeg supermarket in March, 1974.

will be automatically looked after. If after a week or two you find you haven't allotted enough food, increase the amounts of all the per/100 lb. items. For instance, if you were multiplying the *Amounts Required* by 4.5, try multiplying them by 5 instead. Soon you will discover just the right amounts for yourself or your group. The restraints should be taken seriously, but you should not worry about being undernourished. If you feel ill, consult your doctor, get clinical tests done. Get to the bottom of any malaise that you experience. Make any changes in your life necessary to solve your problems, physical, mental, social, spiritual; but please, my friend, enjoy your food.

## Restraints

I will comment briefly on each food or food group on the buying guide and mention any details that you should keep in mind when planning details of your food purchases.

### Grains

Grains here means products such as:

> Whole wheat
> Cracked wheat
> Flour
> Spaghetti and other pasta
> Wheat products
> Rolled oats
>    (large flake or small flake)
> Other oat products
> Rye flour
> Cracked rye
> Whole barley
> Barley meal
> Whole buckwheat
> Cracked buckwheat
> Buckwheat flour
> Buckwheat noodles
> Rice
> * Millet

---

* because of small demand at present, millet can only be found in specialty shops.

# NUTRIENT COMPOSITION OF SOME COMMON GRAINS AND NUTS
## 100 gram portions (about 3½ ounces)

| | Calories | Protein | Fat | Carbohydrate (less fibre) | Calcium | Iron | Vitamin A | Thiamin | Riboflavin | Niacin | Vitamin C |
|---|---|---|---|---|---|---|---|---|---|---|---|
| | | Grams | Grams | Grams | Mg. | Mg. | Iu. | Mg. | Mg. | Mg. | Mg. |
| **MORE NUTRITIOUS GRAINS (raw and dry)** | | | | | | | | | | | |
| Oats, Rolled Oats | 390 | 14.2 | 7.4 | 67.0 | 53 | 4.5 | 0 | .60 | .14 | 1.0 | 0 |
| Wheat, Whole Grain (hard red spring) | | 14.0 | 2.2 | 66.8 | 36 | 3.1 | 0 | .57 | .12 | 4.3 | 0 |
| Whole wheat flour | 333 | 13.3 | 2.0 | 68.7 | 41 | 3.3 | 0 | .55 | .12 | 4.3 | 0 |
| White flour, enriched | 364 | 10.5 | 1.0 | 75.8 | 16 | 2.9 | 0 | .44 | .26 | 3.5 | 0 |
| Rye, whole grain | 334 | 12.1 | 1.7 | 71.4 | 38 | 3.7 | 0 | .43 | .22 | 1.6 | 0 |
| Dark rye flour | 327 | 16.3 | 2.6 | 65.7 | 54 | 4.5 | 0 | .61 | .22 | 2.7 | 0 |
| Buckwheat, whole grain | 335 | 11.7 | 2.4 | 63.0 | 114 | 3.1 | 0 | .60 | [1] | 4.4 | 0 |
| Dark buckwheat flour | 333 | 11.7 | 2.5 | 70.4 | 33 | 2.8 | 0 | .58 | .15 | 2.9 | 0 |
| Millet | 327 | 9.9 | 2.9 | 69.7 | 20 | 6.8 | 0 | .73 | .38 | 2.3 | 0 |
| **LESS NUTRITIOUS GRAINS (raw and dry)** | | | | | | | | | | | |
| Barley, pot or scotch | 348 | 9.6 | 1.1 | 76.3 | 34 | 2.7 | 0 | .21 | .07 | 3.7 | 0 |
| Cornmeal, whole, unbolted | 355 | 9.2 | 3.9 | 72.1 | 20 | 2.4 | 510[2] | .38 | .11 | 2.0 | 0 |
| Cornmeal, enriched | 364 | 7.9 | 1.2 | 77.8 | 6 | 2.9 | 440 | .44 | .26 | 3.5 | 0 |
| Potatoes, 400[4] grams | 304 | 8.4 | .4 | 66.4 | 28 | 2.4 | 20 | .40 | .16 | 6.0 | 80[3] |
| Rice, whole grain, brown | 360 | 7.5 | 1.9 | 76.5 | 32 | 1.6 | 0 | .34 | .05 | 4.7 | 0 |
| **NUTS** | | | | | | | | | | | |
| Almonds | 598 | 19.0 | 54.2 | 16.9 | 234 | 4.7 | 0 | .24[5] | .92 | 3.5 | Trace |
| Brazil nuts | 654 | 14.0 | 66.9 | 7.8 | 186 | 3.4 | Trace | .96[5] | .12 | 1.6 | – |
| Peanuts | 564 | 26.0 | 47.5 | 16.2 | 69 | 2.1 | - | 1.14[5] | .13 | 17.2 | 0 |
| Sunflower seeds | 560 | 24.0 | 47.3 | 16.1 | 120 | 7.1 | 10 | 1.96[5] | .23 | 5.4 | – |
| Walnuts, English | 651 | 14.0 | 64.0 | 17.7 | 99 | 3.1 | 30 | .33[5] | .13 | .9 | 2 |

No figure given in Handbook #8. It should be similar to the figure used for the dark flour.
Yellow varieties – white cornmeal has only a trace.
Year around average - recently dug potatoes 26 mg/100 gm. after 3 months storage half that   after 6 months storage one third that.
Nutrient content of potatoes is shown here with the grains because of their similarity when considered in isocaloric amounts or on a dry weight basis.
Decreases markedly with roasting.
SOURCE: USDA Handbook #8.
Nutritional composition of foods varies with the season, the soil and other factors. Figures in these and other tables represent averages.

There are others not so familiar in North America. Eat a mixture of whole grains or of whole grains and enriched grains. Although an occasional meal of refined unenriched grains would not jeopardize your nutritional standing, their consumption is not recommended on this diet. If you *do* eat white rice, unenriched spaghetti or similar products count it as sugar consumption. Above you will see a chart showing the nutrient contents of the various grains important in our part of the world. Notice the varying nutritive values. For the purposes of this diet, I have divided them into two

## NUTRIENT COMPOSITION OF SOME COMMON LEGUMES
### 100 gram portions raw and dried (about 3½ ounces)

| 100 Gm. raw and dried | Calories | Protein (Gm) | Fat (Gm) | Carbohydrate (Gm) | Calcium (Mg) | Iron (Mg) | Vitamin A (IU) | Thiamin (Mg) | Riboflavin (Mg) | Niacin (Mg) | Ascorbic Acid (Vitamin C) (Mg) |
|---|---|---|---|---|---|---|---|---|---|---|---|
| Beans | | | | | | | | | | | |
| White | 340 | 22.3 | 1.6 | 57.0 | 144 | 7.8 | 0 | .65 | .22 | 2.4 | 0 |
| Red | 343 | 22.5 | 1.5 | 57.7 | 110 | 6.9 | 20 | .51 | .20 | 2.3 | 0 |
| Pinto, Calico, Red Mexican | 349 | 22.9 | 1.2 | 59.4 | 135 | 6.4 | — | .84 | .21 | 2.2 | 0 |
| Lima | 345 | 20.4 | 1.6 | 59.7 | 72 | 7.8 | — | .48 | .17 | 1.9 | 0 |
| Broad beans | 338 | 25.1 | 1.7 | 51.5 | 102 | 7.1 | 70 | .50 | .30 | 2.5 | 0 |
| Soybeans | 403 | 34.1 | 17.7 | 28.6 | 226 | 8.4 | 80 | 1.10 | .31 | 2.2 | 0 |
| Mung beans | 340 | 24.2 | 1.3 | 55.9 | 118 | 7.7 | 80 | .38 | .21 | 2.6 | 0 |
| Mung beans, sprouted, raw | 35 | 3.8 | .2 | 5.9 | 19 | 1.3 | 20 | .13 | .13 | .8 | 19 |
| Peas² | 340 | 24.1 | 1.3 | 55.4 | 64 | 5.1 | 120 | .74 | .29 | 2.0 | 0 |
| Lentils³ | 340 | 24.7 | 1.1 | 56.2 | 79 | 6.8 | 60 | .37 | .22 | 2.0 | 0 |
| Cowpeas including Blackeye peas | 343 | 22.8 | 1.5 | 57.3 | 74 | 5.8 | 30 | 1.05 | .21 | 2.2 | 0 |

¹ Less fiber.
² Split peas very similar
³ Split lentils similar except less calcium
SOURCE: USDA Handbook #8

groups according to nutritional value. At least half your grain quota should come from the "more nutritious grains" group. If you acquire grain products to which sugar or fat have been added, such as breads or cakes, make sure you count any sugar or fat contained therein as such and not as part of your grain quota. If the product is very fat or very sweet count it entirely as fat or sugar.

Potatoes, on a dry weight basis contain amounts of nutrients similar to less nutritious grains and can be used interchangeably with them. Buy four times the amount of potatoes as that of grain you are replacing. You will be getting extra vitamin C in the bargain, but the body handles it well so it is no disadvantage.

If you increase the amount of less nutritious grains beyond half the total grains, treat the excess as sugar.

Nuts, sunflower seeds and sesame seeds may be considered as part of the grain quota, but if used in large amounts, half their weight should be counted as fat.

*Grains provide calories, protein, iron, thiamin, and niacin.*

## Legumes

In French, legumes means vegetables; here it means mature beans, peas, lentils. *Legumes furnish similar nutrients to grains. They provide more iron and more protein than grains and the protein is of a higher biological value.*

## Skim milk powder

Either instant or non-instant may be used. Non-instant skimmed milk powder is harder to find, harder to mix, but of better flavour than the instant. The only reason skimmed milk powder is recommended over other milk products is its low cost. However, it is handy to use in yeast breads and fermented milk products because it doesn't require scalding before use. Since it keeps well, especially in cold temperature, it can be bought in bulk if this is an advantage. The .7 lb skimmed milk powder per week called for in the *Weekly Food List* is about 1½ cups liquid milk per day. *Vitamins A and D* ae now added to some brands of skim milk powder. Check the package for this information. *Skim milk powder* *provides most of the calcium and riboflavin in this diet. It provides calories, protein of high biological value, thiamin, niacin, and vitamin $B_{12}$.*

### Eggs

Buy the most economical size. I'll stop right here to help you get an idea of "how much egg is one egg?" In Canada, legal weights for eggs are:

| | |
|---|---|
| Small | 1½ oz. each |
| Medium | 1¾ oz. each |
| Large | 2  oz. each |
| Extra large | 2¼ oz. each |

When eggs cost about 50¢/dozen of mediums, a 7¢ price spread is reasonable. That is: smalls should cost 43¢; large should cost 57¢, Extra large should cost about 64¢. (You can get a "Ready Reckoner" Egg Price Chart from the Canada Department of Agriculture which will show you the exact "reasonable price spread" for eggs of different sizes.) The higher the egg price, the greater the reasonable spread in prices. Many people buy mediums regardless of the price of different size eggs – recipes call for them. The price per egg is less than the larger eggs and "the smalls look so little and funny." Mediums are seldom the best buy.

The buying guide calls for 7 medium eggs per person. That's 12 ounces of eggs (counting the shell). You don't have to buy "medium" eggs. Just make sure you get 12 ounces of eggs. To do this, divide 12 by the weight/egg of the different sizes and round off to the nearest egg. You get these equivalents:

8 Small Eggs = 7 Medium Eggs = 6 Large Eggs = 5 Extra Large Eggs. *Eggs furnish calories, protein of high biological value, iron, vitamin A, thiamin, riboflavin, niacin, vitamin $B_{12}$.*

### Vegetables

The cabbage, potatoes, carrots, rutabagas provide small amounts of various nutrients. See pages 132 and 133. You will notice that they are the main source of vitamin C on this diet. Buy fresh, firm, crisp ones. Treat them with respect.

Store them in covered containers or plastic bags in the refrigerator. Eat them raw or cook them briefly using any cooking liquid in soups and sauces.

Hold on a minute – I've just tossed off one of those bits of casual, half-sound advice. If you have a minute, lets go into the question of vitamin C.

Ascorbic Acid (vitamin C) is different from other vitamins in that it oxidizes very quickly. (You know about oxidation; when a nail becomes rusty it has oxidized. Some of the metal has reacted with oxygen from the air and has become a different compound, namely, iron rust.) A potato, for instance, when it is freshly dug has about 28 mg. vitamin C per 100 grams potato. Store the potato 3 months and the vitamin C will have decreased to about 20 mg. If you bake the potato until it is just done, it still has about 20 mg. vitamin C. If you boil it briefly and throw away the water the potato has about 15 mg. vitamin C. If you mash it until it is light and fluffy more vitamin C is lost. If you leave it over night and hash brown it the next day, you shouldn't count it as a source of vitamin C.

The same is true of other vegetables and fruits. Cabbage retains vitamin C better through storage. Tomatoes retain it better during cooking and subsequent storage. If you begin to get nervous about vitamin C, you are following a well established tradition. Have faith. Be reasonable.

Eating the per person amounts of vegetables raw, or baked in the case of potato, you should get around 40 mg. vitamin C per day. That's twice the British recommendation and 33% more than the Canadian Dietary Standard – not an excess, but ample. If I had no other sources of vitamin C than .6 lbs. cabbage, rutabaga turnips, carrots and 1 lb. of potatoes per week, I would eat them raw or maybe bake the potato or make potato soup or stir-fry one or two minutes, Chinese-style. On days that I ate a half an orange or some strips of green pepper or some grapefruit wedges or drank some well steeped rose-hip tea I would feel quite free to fry my potatoes or even (mon dieu!) drain and mash my turnips. Vitamins are not tempermental deities that we have to appease, but ordinary chemical compounds which our bodies happen to need. Learn the facts.

Carrots, along with butter or fortified margarine provide most of the vitamin A value of this diet. Fruits and vegetables do not contain vitamin A. However carotenes and other vegetable pigments found in dark green and yellow vegetables and in some fruits can be *used* by the body to make vitamin A. The degree of absorption of these carotenes varies widely. Sometimes as much as 75% is lost in the digestive process.* *The Canadian Dietary Standard* recommendation of 3,700 IU vitamin A per day per adult assumes that half that amount, 1,850 IU, will be preformed vitamin A. This is the reason for the per person quota of butter or fortified margarine in the *Weekly Food List*. If you expect to get all your vitamin A value from vegetable sources, you would need to get 7,400 IU per day per adult.

## Fats

Fats here refer to margarine, butter, rendered animal fats, edible oils, half the weight of nuts eaten in large amounts, and foods which are mainly oil or other fat such as potato chips. I will not open a discussion as to the comparative desirability of different fats. It is a question that the researchers have not settled. Watch for factual information and prod researchers and government bodies for action. Fats provide calories. Butter and fortified margarine are depended on to provide vitamin A (see above). Although no minimum requirement for fat has been established, some fatty acids are essential to the body. The Canadian Dietary Standard states that 25% of the calories in a diet come from fat. Fat makes up nearly 40% of the calories of Canadian diets (see page 129.) This diet derives about 25% of its calories from fats.

## Sugars

Any food which contributes mainly sugar to the diet is here classed as sugar. This includes white sugar, brown sugar, syrups, honey, molasses, sweetened drinks, candy, cookies, cakes, dried fruits, and many packaged sweetened things. Sugars contribute calories to the diet. Dried fruits also contribute some iron. Dark molasses contributes iron and cal-

---

* Canadian Council on Nutrition, *Canadian Bulletin on Nutrition*, Vol. 6, No. 1, Information Canada, March, 1964.

# NUTRIENT COMPOSITION OF SOME COMMON SUGARS
## 100 gram portions (about 3½ ounces)

| FOOD | Calories | Protein Gm. | Fat Gm. | Carbohydrate (less fibre) Gm. | Calcium Mg. | Iron Mg. | Vitamin A IU | Thiamin Mg. | Riboflavin Mg. | Niacin Mg. | Vitamin C |
|---|---|---|---|---|---|---|---|---|---|---|---|
| White sugar | 385 | 0 | 0 | 99.5 | 0 | .1 | 0 | 0 | 0 | 0 | 0 |
| Brown sugar | 373 | 0 | 0 | 96.4 | 85 | 3.4 | 0 | .01 | .03 | .2 | 0 |
| Honey | 304 | .3 | 0 | 82.3 | 5 | .5 | 0 | Trace | .04 | .3 | 1 |
| Molasses: | | | | | | | | | | | |
| 1st extraction (light) | 252 | - | - | 65. | 167 | 4.3 | - | .07 | .06 | .2 | - |
| 2nd extraction (medium) | 232 | - | - | 60. | 290 | 6.0 | - | - | .12 | 1.2 | - |
| 3rd extraction (Black-strap) | 213 | - | - | 55. | 684 | 16.1 | - | .11 | .19 | 2.0 | - |
| Barbados | 271 | - | - | 70. | 245 | 6.0 | - | .06 | .20 | - | - |
| Sorghum | 257 | 0 | 0 | 68. | 172 | 12.5 | - | - | .10 | .1 | - |
| Dates | 274 | 2.2 | .5 | 70.6 | 59 | 3.0 | 50 | .09 | .10 | 2.2 | 0 |
| Figs | 274 | 4.3 | 1.3 | 63.5 | 126 | 3.0 | 80 | .10 | .10 | .7 | 0 |
| Prunes | 255 | 2.1 | .6 | 65.8 | 51 | 3.9 | 1600 | .09 | .17 | 1.6 | 3 |
| Raisins (unbleached) | 289 | 2.5 | .2 | 76.5 | 62 | 3.5 | 20 | .11 | .08 | .5 | 1 |

(Dash indicates lack of reliable data for a constituent believed to be present in measurable amounts.)
SOURCE: USDA Handbook #8.

cium. Sugars serve as a recipe ingredient and lend interest and flavour to other foods.

Abundant supplies of refined sugar became available in the 19th century and added to the aesthetic qualitites of tea cakes and other dainties and to the tooth decay of so called civilized peoples. High consumption of refined sugar also has an effect on the incidence of obesity, diabetes, heart disease and mal-nutrition in a population. Whether its use has meant an increase or decrease in the general quality of life is certainly debatable.

This diet does not depend on sugars for nutrients so you can make your own decision as to whether to eat white sugar, honey, or molasses or no sugar at all on your porridge.

I have no enthusiasm for white sugar. It adds sweetness – nothing more. Nutritionally, it adds calories – nothing more. Honey, in contrast, adds beautiful flavour and small amounts of minerals and vitamins. Molasses adds hearty flavour and useful amounts of iron and calcium.

When you stop using white sugar, and stop sweetening things so heavily, you will be surprised to find that all kinds of things have subtle sweetening qualities. Raisins, dates, oranges, onions, baked squash are sweet and impart a haunt-ing sweetness (as well as valuable nutrients) to other foods. It's nothing but good news!

**Miscellaneous**

This is an important group of items on this or any diet – the handful of salty black olives and the little chunk of Feta cheese that taste so good with the plate of red beans. This is the onions that go well with every item on the list. This is the salt, the basil, the oregano, the yeast, the red apple to brighten a bag-lunch or a midnight vigil.

A sound practice in buying food and planning meals is to demand that each food serves more than one purpose. As far as possible, I buy foods which are pretty to look at, fragrant, delicious, fun to eat and nourishing. Thus a fresh pineapple graces the table and scents the room while it ripens, turns an ordinary snack into a special occasion and has vitamin C to boot. Cut a lemon in half. With your bare hands, squeeze the juice into a pot of soup or a salad. Squeeze it hard to expel all the juice and part of the lemon oils. Now cup your hand over your nose and sniff. Such a joy. When I do the same with a lime, I have to take a five minute break to sit and sniff the lime. Cut an orange in half, then quarters. Cut each quarter into three pieces. Pass the dozen bite size chunks around in close company. It is a very friendly thing to do.

## Vitamin D

Children and pregnant or lactating women should ingest 400 IU of vitamin D daily. This is to insure against deficiency caused by lack of sunshine on the skin. Foods on the *Weekly Food List* may or may not provide this amount of vitamin D value. Check labels of milk products to estimate the amount your children are getting. You may need to buy a vitamin D supplement for them especially if they are not getting out in the sunshine several times a week. Do not exceed recommended dosage, as excess of vitamin D preparations can have undesirable side effects.

## Deletions, Additions, Substitutions, Adjustments

The only deletion you can make from the foods on the *Weekly Food List* without sacrificing nutrients is sugar. You may add foods in small amounts such as seasonings or a piece of fruit. Foods with few calories such as mushrooms, cranberries, tomatoes, cucumbers, green leafy vegetables you may add as you wish and can afford. Most changes are actually substitutions. You must make substitutions carefully. Make sure that the foods you are introducing contribute nutrients similar to the ones that you are leaving off.
As a rule of thumb:

Count any fats or sugars as part of your fat or sugar quota.
Add other foods up to 200 calories per day without making any adjustment in your total diet.
If you add foods containing more than 200 calories per day, check their nutritive value and the nutritive value of the foods they are displacing. Make sure the foods added furnish amounts of essential nutrients equal to or better than those foods being replaced.

Thus, lean meats, eggs and legumes can be substituted for grain. Meat and eggs can be substituted for legumes. Whole milk can be substituted for skim milk powder (count the butterfat as part of your fat allowance). To make a substitution for eggs requires a mixture of foods for the egg is unique in its array and concentration of essential nutrients. Foods high in fat such as potato chips, bacon, olives, commercial salad dressings, nuts, cream, cream cheese can be substituted for fat. If you choose not to eat butter or margarine, special care must be taken to insure adequate intakes of vitamin A and essential fatty acids.

People ask me about protein quality and quantity on this diet. (Please see the chart on page 134 for weekly nutrient intakes of persons following the Weekly Food list compared to the Canadian Dietary Standard for each person.) I figured probable nutrient intakes for people of varying sizes as well as people with very high nutrient requirements. In nearly every case a person would get twice his suggested intake of protein, which is more than enough to make up for the relatively low biological value of some of the vegetable proteins.

The very interesting question of protein needs and protein sources is too involved to treat thoroughly here. Don't be cowed when the term "incomplete protein" is used to describe vegetables, grains and nuts. The term seems to indicate that vegetable proteins are totally lacking in something. This is not true. Scientists rate proteins on different scales. One scale, Net Protein Utilization, represents the extent to which food eaten is converted into body tissue. Egg and human breast milk are used most efficiently. They are designated as having an NPU of 100.

| Food | NPU |
|------|-----|
| Human Breast Milk | 100 |
| Whole Egg | 100 |
| Cow's Milk | 75 |
| Beef Muscle | 80 |
| Beef Liver | 65 |
| Fish | 83 |
| Rice | 57 |
| Peanut Flour | 48 |
| Soy Flour | 56 |
| Sunflour Seed | 65 |
| Potato | 71 |
| Navy Bean | 47 |

These figures are related only to protein quality, not to the quantity of protein in a food.
Source: FAO/WHO Expert Group, *World Health Organization Technical Report, Series No. 301*, Rome, 1965.

This means that one must eat larger amounts of vegetable proteins than of animal proteins. Various vegetable proteins are low in different amino acids. One that is low in methionine/cystine may be high in tryptophan. If this food is eaten with a food that is high in methionine/cystine and low in tryptophan, the mixture is then a better source of both amino acids than either food alone. This effect is called "mutual supplementation." It is reasonable to eat foods together which mutually supplement each other.

## Some Mutually Supplementary Foods

    Legumes and cereals
    Sesame Seeds and corn
    Sesame Seeds and legumes
    Sesame Seeds and peanuts
    Coconut and rice
    Coconut and peanuts
    Sunflower Seeds and legumes
    Sunflower Seeds and peanuts

Source: Swaminathan, M. "The Availability of Plant Proteins" Vol. 3, Chapter 4, *Newer Methods of Nutritional Biochemistry*, Edited by A. A. Albanese, Academic Press, NY, 1965.

See *Diet for a Small Planet* by Frances Moore Lappé, Ballantine Books, NY, 1971, for a detailed examination of the effect of mutual supplementation of vegetable proteins and recipes to help make it all happen.

If someone in your group has special needs, you will have to make some adjustments when estimating food requirements. Any fast growing person whether child, pregnant or lactating woman or someone doing unaccustomed physical work and building muscles will need more food than his weight would indicate. This can generally be accommodated by multiplying the per 100 lb. stuffs by a higher figure. A pregnant or nursing woman is actually eating for herself and for a baby. Figure for her 1½ times the per person stuffs and the per child skimmed milk powder.

This diet is meant for anyone able to chew, digest, and metabolize the foods listed.

Here you have a basic list of resources from which to plan your very good but very cheap diet. Look back over the list –

grains, beans, skim milk powder, eggs, fats, sugars, vegetables: it will take some planning. Plan now!

## How to Convert the Weekly Food List into Meals and Snacks for People to Eat

So you want to try something new! Whether changing your mind is the hard part or the easy part of development is subject to debate. I'll try to give you some techniques that will help you get the change into action. You will need to:

1. Define your aims, resources, and special requirements
2. Make a meal plan
3. Make a menu
4. Check the menu

If you are successful, you will have become a better decision-maker and a more contented customer.

## Define Aims, Resources, and Special Requirements

We will continue using the Sample Family for demonstration (see Weekly Food List made out for them on page 32.)

After searching discussion, the Sample Family recorded the following:

*Aims in order of priority*

- to eat in joy
- to get enough of each essential nutrient
- to eat simply
- to eat unrefined foods
- to cut sugar consumption very low
- to eat cheaply

*Resources*

- Mother likes to make bread and yogurt
- Teenage son can make very good granola
- Everyone is willing to try a new style of eating

*Special requirements*

- Easy preparation meals when possible

46

## Make a Meal Plan

A constant supply of nourishing instant foods will insure that a good snack or small meal can be prepared by child or adult at any time. These "Ever-Readies" can also be used to supplement a meal that is too small for someone's needs.

*Ever-Readies*

| | |
|---|---|
| good bread | cabbage |
| margarine | carrots |
| peanut butter | rutabaga turnips |
| cheeses | nuts |
| honey | rolled oats |
| molasses | unsweetened coconut |
| yogurt | sesame seeds |
| granola | sunflower seeds |
| skimmed milk powder | wheat germ |
| canned and frozen juices | eggs |
| fresh or dried fruits | |

*Breakfast*

Porridge + Ever-Readies

*Lunch*

Something from previous dinner + Ever-Readies

*Dinner*

Soup (if possible)
Bean or Whole Grain Main Course
Potato (often)
Cooked Vegetable or Salad
Dessert (occasionally)

## Make a Menu

— See suggested sample menu page 48. For detailed menu of the 2 week test diet see appendix pages 136 to 139.

— Make a grocery list of any item not on hand.

# Sample Weekly Menu

| | Monday | Tuesday | Wednesday | Thursday | Friday | Saturday | Sunday |
|---|---|---|---|---|---|---|---|
| **Breakfast** | Choice of Porridge or Ever-Readies | | | | | Nutty Pancakes Yogurt and Blueberry Sauce | Raisin Muffins Cheese Slices Grapefruit Sections |
| **Lunch** | Leftovers or Ever-Readies | | | | | *Minestrone Soup *Whole Grain Bread Cheese Slices or Peanut Butter | *Baked Beans Bread and Margarine Cabbage Leaf Apple Pie |
| **Dinner** | Steamed Mixed Grains with Yogurt Baked Potatoes with Chopped Onions *Cabbage & Almonds Baked Custard | *Basic Beans Potatoes in their skins *Sabzi Cabbage Leaf | *Dutch Bean Soup *Spaghetti/Tomato Sauce Grated Cheese *Tossed Salad *Chinese Chews | *Lentil Loaf Mashed Potatoes *Florentine Beans Turnip Sticks Orange Wedges | *French Onion Soup *Parsley Rice Baked Potato Waldorf Salad | *Baked Beans Potato Salad *Cabbage Salad with Blue Cheese *Boston Brown Bread Apple Pie & Cheese | *Curried Vegetables Curried Eggs Brown Rice *Chutney Chipatti Bananas in Yogurt |

* These dishes can be found in the recipe section

- Make sure sources of iron, calcium, Vitamin A, vitamin C are represented daily.

- Is labour available to do the cooking required?

- Make a note of pre-preparation needed; e.g., "Tuesday night – Soak beans."

**Special Note**

Each member of the family should appreciate the need to eat foods containing iron, calcium, vitamin A, vitamin C and protein. (If not consuming any meat, milk or eggs regularly, he must take special care to insure adequate amounts of vitamin $B_{12}$ and riboflavin.) Any person eating his or her share of the foods on the Weekly Food List should receive ample amounts of all nutrients. But by the time a child is eight or ten years old in our society he or she is eating snacks and meals away from home.

*The skill of choosing nourishing foods is as important to a child as the skill of crossing the street properly or dressing warmly in winter.*

**How to Plan an Intelligent Diet for One Person**

I have been asked frequently, "How would you plan a 50¢/day diet for one person? It looks easy for a group, but it would be impossible for a person living alone." So for kicks, here's how I would feed myself.

I would plan a very simple eating routine because I wouldn't want to spend a lot of time on personal upkeep. I would have a large bowl of rolled oat porridge for breakfast. For lunch I would have either muesli or bread, margarine and bean paste. I would plan to eat a cabbage leaf or two and a carrot each day as a nibbler while working. I would also plan ½ pound raw peanuts and ½ pound raisins as nibblers per week. For supper, I would make a vegetable stew or simple bean dish. For dessert, I would have a thick slice of bread and molasses or yogurt and fruit.

You can see from the *Weekly Food List* (page 50) that I have made several of the adjustments mentioned in the restraints. I increased the amount of potatoes and counted them as part of my grain allowance (1 pound potatoes = ¼

## WEEKLY FOOD LIST

Name of person or group    Caroline's Bachelor Diet    Date    1974

Number of Adults _____ Number of Children _____

Weight of person or group 100 lbs.    Weekly Food Budget    $4.50

| Food | Amounts Required | Amounts To Buy lb | Price per lb | Cost |
|---|---|---|---|---|
| Grains | 4.0 lb/100 lb | 4 | $ * | $1.15 |
| Legumes | .5 lb/100 lb | .5 | .40 | .20 |
| Skim Milk Powder | .7 lb/100 lb | .7 | .60 | .42 |
| Eggs | 7 Medium/person | 7 eggs | .07 | .49 |
| Vegetables | | | | |
| Cabbage | .6 lb/person | 1.0 | .12 | .12 |
| Carrots | .6 lb/person | 1.0 | .13 | .13 |
| Potatoes | 1.0 lb/person | * | | |
| Rutabagas | .6 lb/person | .6 | .10 | .06 |
| Fats | | | | |
| Total fats | .8 lb/100 lb | .8 | * | .24 |
| Butter or fortified margarine | .5 lb/adult | .5 | | |
| Other fats | | .3 | * | |
| Sugars | .8 lb/100 lb | .8 | – | .23 |
| Total Cost for Basics | | | | 3.04 |
| Miscellaneous | | | * | .82 |
| Total Weekly Food Budget | $4.50 | Surplus $ .64 | | 3.86 |

\* See details, page 51

---

pound less nutritious grain). I assumed I could get a good buy on skimmed milk powder. You can see this is quite a liberal diet. I included more expensive items in nearly every category. The amounts of miscellaneous items I added were small so that displacement of buying guide items need not be a concern (nutrition wise) – I have 41¢ left over for a fund to buy spices, yeast, yogurt starter, etc. The only cooking I would have to do would be boiling porridge – and a little vegetable stew or variation and my .5 pound of beans.

I would trade services on the bread and yogurt. I would do a large batch each week and would trade off with someone for transportation or something like that.

**DETAIL SHEET**   Name   <u>**Caroline's Bachelor Diet**</u>

| Food Category | Specific Food | Amount to buy lb | Price Per lb | Cost |
|---|---|---|---|---|
| **Grains** | Whole Wheat Flour | 1.5 | $ .17 | $ .26 |
| | Rolled Oats | 1.25 | .23 | .29 |
| | Potatoes (½ lb dry wt.) | 2.00 | .08 | .16 |
| | Peanuts (¼ lb oil) | .5 | .88 | .44 |
| | | | | 1.15 |
| | | | | |
| **Legumes** | A variety | .5 | .40 | .20 |
| | | | | |
| **Fats .8 lb.** | Margarine | .5 | .39 | .20 |
| | Vegetable Oil | .1 | .40 | .04 |
| | Oil from Peanuts | .2 | Charged above | |
| | | | | .24 |
| | | | | |
| **Sugars .8 lb.** | Dates | .3 | .30 | .09 |
| | Molasses | .5 | .28 | .14 |
| | | | | .23 |
| | | | | |
| **Miscellaneous** | Onions | .5 | .20 | .10 |
| | Black Olives | .2 | 1.00 | .20 |
| | Canned Tomatoes | .5 | .24 | .12 |
| | Fruit | | | .40 |
| | | | | .82 |

These are supermarket prices as of March, 1974.

---

## Become a Decision Maker

Look again at the Weekly Food Lists and detail sheets of Sample Family and Caroline's Bachelor Diet. Notice that most of the foods are simple, basic commodities. They can be stored in a very small space. The tiniest refrigerator will house the few "keep cold" items. With such a simple grocery list, the supermarket with its multimillion decisions and pressures will pose no problem to you. The foods are very cheap.

Suddenly you have a manageable list of items to consider, 25 – 30 instead of the usual 200. Perhaps you can start to exert the force of your own will on the selection of foods.

51

Could you deal directly with a producer for some items? Would a consumer co-op be useful in expressing your priorities to the food industry? Give it some thought. You're bound to win.

## Some Effects of Change

Changing from a Typical North American Diet to a diet of less meat, less fat, less sugar and other refined foods, less packaged, processed and expensive foods will have some effects on your life. You will save cash. You will learn to cook or eat very simply. You will become acquainted with flavours you never knew existed.

You may experience a change in your digestion. You will probably have more intestinal gas and a larger volume of stool (possibly even quite soft at first). Within 2 or 3 weeks your body should have made the adjustment nicely. After 2 years of eating mainly the foods on the Weekly Food List, I still marvel at the great comfort of my digestion and at the feeling of well-being I feel after a meal.

At first you may have to give special attention to eating enough food. Less fat and refined sugar (which are very concentrated sources of calories) means that you will require a larger total volume of food. However the extra chewing required to eat less refined foods tends to have a satisfying effect.

As you eat less sugar and depend more on natural foods to sweeten things (a small amount of honey, a handful of raisins, some dates, slices of apple or orange) you may find your perception of sweetness changes. I keep cutting back on the sugar of recipes and increasing the truly flavourful ingredients.

You may notice a change in your complexion. My teenage son stopped eating sugar altogether as a result of a radio talk he heard. Three weeks later he was surprised to find that his facial blemishes had gone away.

After you have had the experience for days or weeks of enjoying subtle natural flavours of simple good foods it will be hard to go back. A bakery lemon bun or soft macaroni may repulse you.

After a while of thoughtfully chewing and being sensitive to taste and smell and texture you will notice all kinds of sensations you never knew existed.

So I find myself saying to the man at the supermarket, "What was the matter with the cabbage last week. It was bitter and left kind of a burning sensation in my mouth."

"Lady, you are a trouble maker!" the manager answers. "The cabbage was cabbage like all other cabbages."

I realize he is sincere. He probably wouldn't have noticed any difference had he tasted my bitter cabbage head. I wouldn't have either two years ago. I will notice the difference from now on.

## How I've Changed

My attitudes towards this material have changed in the 2 years that I have been working with it. At the start it was: "Wow, what a lot of really fine meals you can have without eating meat. How truly satisfying! How amazingly cheap! Are they nutritionally adequate according to North American standards?" I still feel these things. The question of nutritional adequacy has been answered to my satisfaction.

My attitude now is: It behooves us humans to become friendly with the earth on which we live, its air, its rivers and lakes, its forests and grasslands, its tiny creatures, its large animals of which you and I are two – to learn to understand and appreciate the chemical, physical, spiritual elements that go together to make up life. And in so doing we will learn to extract our own living from the totality of life in ways which are considerate, which are least destructive and most generative of life.

I wish you well.

There follows recipes for a few of the very many truly wonderful dishes you can make from inexpensive foods.

# PART THREE

# A SMALL SELECTION
# OF
# UNIQUE RECIPES

# INTRODUCTION

Herein you will find a few ideas for making really delicious foods from the cheapest of ingredients. Expensive items are used here and there in very small amounts for flavouring.

Some recipes are still experimental (Cheese 'N Yogurt Pie isn't perfected yet); some recipes are valuable. (The Italian Spaghetti Sauce and the Whole Wheat Bread recipe are each worth the price of the book.)

Get into this cooking thing. The rewards are so fine! I just wandered into the kitchen for, maybe a cup of coffee. I was feeling a little tired. Once there, I remembered the pot I had left simmering. To the liquid drained from supper vegetables, I added green pepper stems and cabbage cores and parsley stems saved in the freezer in a little bag and a clove of garlic. I found it all nicely done so I drained the soup off the vegetable parts and added a couple tablespoons tomato paste, a tsp vinegar, salt, pepper and a shake of garlic powder. I returned it to a boil to insure against spoilage and poured myself a cupful. With increasing enthusiasm I opened some cracker tins and found an oat cake and a couple of rye crackers (recipes, page 68). Ahhh! Such utter pleasure.

## Cooking notes

### 1.  Fats and Oils

In some recipes, I have indicated "oil" or "fat." I will try to describe the attributes of different fats and oils to help you choose the one you want for a particular purpose

#### LARD

The rendered fat of hogs. Has limited shortening power. Will combine with flour in proportions as high as 1:3. Some people value the flavour of pastry made with it. Its flavour does not compete with that of butter so that a lard and butter combination in pastry, cookies, cakes is possible. Works well for greasing baking pans. Shelf life a few months. Price is quite low.

### SHORTENING

Can be made from lard or a mixture of lard and vegetable fats. It has been treated to enhance its "shortening" and keeping qualities.

### ALL VEGETABLE SHORTENING

Made from hydrogenated vegetable fats. Has better combining power than lard in baked products. To get the lightest cakes and the tenderest crispiest cookies you must use shortening. Imparts no flavour of its own to a product. Good for greasing.

### SPECIAL PASTRY SHORTENING

Used by the baking trade for its especially high shortening power. Can be used with flour in proportions of 1:2. It has made possible cheap puff pastry and never-fail very crisp tender cookies as well as the lightest tenderest cakes. It has a high plasticity which means it can be formed and shaped easily.

### BUTTER

Shortening power about the same as lard. Good taste. Expensive. There is a great variation in butter flavour though most of us aren't aware of it.

## Vegetable Oils

Vegetable oils have been the traditional cooking fat in many countries. In North America they have achieved prominence with the advent of efficient seed milling technology and popular concern about fat intake and heart disease.

Oil gives a different result in baking than solid fat. A special recipe is required for substitution in cakes, cookies.

Where amounts of fat are relatively small such as in yeast breads, quick breads, pancakes, oil may be substituted without changing amounts of other ingredients.

For frying and salad dressings, flavour is an important factor. People have strong feelings about which oil they like best. When I can, I use olive oil for Mediterranean dishes, peanut oil (the Chinese kind is the tastiest) for Chinese food and rape seed oil for general purpose.

## 2. Flours

I haven't always specified what kind of flour to use in the recipes. It depends on your aims and what you can get. I will try to explain the attributes of different kinds of flour and you can make your own decisions.

### CAKE AND PASTRY FLOUR

Made from soft wheat – poor for bread making. Makes light, tender cakes. If you want to make cakes 50% whole wheat, 50% white flour, cake flour gives a very nice result.

### ALL PURPOSE FLOUR

This is made from hard wheat after the bran and outer parts of the wheat berry have been removed. Makes a light loaf of bread, a passable cake.

### STRONG BAKERS FLOUR

If you plan to bake bread and can buy from a mill you should consider this flour. It is higher in protein than all purpose flour. It makes good white bread. Mix it with whole wheat or rye flour if you want whole wheat flavour and nourishment, and a high porous loaf.

### UNBLEACHED FLOUR

Some mills make a very high protein flour from the outer most parts of the wheat berry but with no germ or bran. It is unbleached – a creamy color. The mills sell it to bakeries for dark bread products such as rye bread, Hollywood bread.

That sold in supermarkets is white flour with bran added back in. They make it this way because it is little extra bother from the ordinary milling operation. If you want wheat germ you have to add it yourself.

STONE GROUND FLOUR

One local mill that I know of makes a straight run flour for special large orders. That is, they grind the wheat, germ, bran, shorts and all. This is usually sold only in health food stores and is quite expensive. *Real* stone ground flour has to be made in a special mill by a costly process.

## 3. Chemical Leavening Agents

Sodium bicarbonate (baking soda), reacts with acid giving off a carbon dioxide gas and forming a salt. In baking, before the gas has a chance to rise to the top and escape, the batter or dough cooks around it leaving a little hole in the cookie or pancake and making it airy and tender to chew. Sour milk, fruit juice, brown sugar, molasses, vinegar, cream of tartar can provide the acid needed for such a reaction. The problem is how much buttermilk or fruit juice is needed for 1 tsp of soda?

It is a hard question to answer because some buttermilk is more sour (more acid) than other buttermilk and some fruit juice is more acid than other fruit juice. If too little acid is available for the soda to react with, the soda that is left turns the flour yellowish and makes the biscuit or cake taste strong and bad.

This is why baking powder was invented. Exactly the right amount of cream of tartar (tartaric acid made from grapes) was mixed with sodium bicarbonate for complete reaction. Add water—puff—no acid left, no soda left. There was still a problem. The "puff" happened too fast. Before an inexperienced cook could get the cake into the oven, the bubbles of carbon dioxide were coming out the top of the batter. The cake wasn't as light as it should be.

Calcium phosphate was used for the acid. This helped because it gave a slower puff. But some cooks are very slow and the bubbles still escaped. The perfect solution was found in a "double acting baking powder." Mono calcium phosphate or other phosphate and sodium aluminum sulphate were added for the acid. One made bubbles in the mixing bowl; the other made bubbles only when heated. No one could fail now except for one little thing. This baking powder has a strong taste. Unless you put something in the biscuit or muffin to cover it up, you can taste baking powder in the finished product. Pearl Ackerman, the grandmother and Grand Wizer of our family said to me, "You should use 'Magic Baking Powder' because it tastes better." I looked at her with some contempt. Grand Wizers are always making such statements. But last spring when we were trying to develop a party quality whole wheat cake, we taste-tested cakes made with Magic Baking Powder (single action) and cakes made with double action baking powder. There really is a big difference. The cake made with single action baking powder (calcium phosphate and sodium bicarbonate) tasted better.

### 4. Sugars

White sugar, brown sugar, demerara brown sugar may be used interchangeably in most recipes. (Before substituting white sugar for brown check the recipes to see if brown sugar is depended on to provide acid for leavening as explained in note 3, above.) Honey, syrup, molasses, maple syrup may generally be substituted for sugar that is called for in small amounts as in breads, muffins, pancakes. One cup of honey equals 1¼ cups of sugar plus ¼ cup liquid. If the sugar is depended on for structural effects in the end product as in cakes and cookies, liquid carbohydrates may not work at all or may work only with recipe adjustments. Baked products come out heavier when sweetened with honey or molasses.

# BREADS

When eating an inexpensive diet, bread assumes importance. When you learn to bake nourishing, satisfying bread your problem of how to eat well cheaply is half solved. After several weeks of eating your own good bread you will be surprised at how awful the commercial bread you took for granted for so long really tastes.

## Whole Wheat Bread, How To Make It

I developed this recipe over the years making bread for Jerry and the kids. My aim was a recipe that would be easy to remember, simple and fast to mix and scrumptious to eat, crusty on the outside, light and airy on the inside.

To bake this bread properly, you've got to assume a stance. Roll up your sleeves. Wash your hands. Get out a large bowl or a pot, a tablespoon and a teaspoon. You are a baker. Into your charge is given all the lovely ingredients including the yeast, which is a lot of tiny plants, and depends totally on you for its needs. Give it the nourishment of flour and eggs and sugar and provide it with a warm (85 degree F.) moist place to rise away from cool drafts and it will grow and grow for you. The flour is depending on you too, to knead it until its gluten has developed a fine elasticity.

If possible, find a counter or a table the proper height to work on. (To determine this, stand in front of the table with your arm stretched out at a 45 degree angle. If the heel of your hand rests on the table, it is the right height for you.) Now to knead your bread, spread your feet apart so that your weight rests easily on them and your arms and shoulders can move freely. You must put the muscle of your arms and shoulders and the weight of your body into the kneading of your bread. Flour your hands and push the heel of one or both (depending on the amount of dough) into the center. With the fingers pull the edges of the dough up and into the center and turn the dough slightly. Continue until the dough is smooth and springy. It's the growth of the yeast and the elasticity of the flour protein that will give you the light, airy loaf you want. You don't have to fret and worry in making this bread. A little bit more or less of any ingredient won't spoil it. The measurements are given in rounded spoonsful instead of level ones. They are easier to measure quickly.

# WHOLE WHEAT BREAD
## Yield: 3 Large Loaves

Sprinkle

**2 tsp active dry yeast**

On

**½ cup lukewarm water**
**1 tsp sugar**

Stir and set aside. Put in large bowl

**2 tbs lard***
**2 cups hot water**
**2/3 cup skim milk powder**
**2 tbs brown sugar**
**2 tsp salt**
**2 eggs****
**2 cups all purpose flour**

Beat with large spoon till lukewarm. Add yeast mixture.
Add stirring with spoon then with hand

**Whole wheat flour to make a firm dough (about 6 cups)**

Turn out onto a floured not-too-smooth surface and knead vigorously 10 to 20 minutes until the dough is smooth and springy. If the mixing bowl isn't too mucky, put the dough back into it; cover with a damp cloth and set to rise in a warm (85 degrees F.) moist place. (If the proofing place is quite moist with no drafts, the cloth is unnecessary.) In 1½ to 2 hours, when the dough has risen high in the bowl or pan and looks stretched and thin on top, it has risen fully. Punch it down and scrape away any dough sticking to the sides. Turn it again onto the floury surface. Cut it into portions according to the number of loaves you want. Let rest for 10 minutes. Grease your pans, with a solid unsalted fat. Make loaves by: 1) rolling out the dough with a rolling pin and then folding or rolling into loaves, or: 2) by kneading each portion enough to squeeze out any large air bubbles (else you will end with holey bread and the jam will fall through) and shaping into loaves. For a smooth perfect looking loaf, bring the ragged edges to the bottom leaving the top smooth. Let rise again until double in bulk or a little more if you like and bake in a 350 degree F. oven for one hour more or less depending on the

---

* See cooking note #1, page 56

** Eggs called for are assumed to be medium size unless otherwise stated. In flexible recipes such as this one any size egg may be used. In a less flexible one such as cakes or cookies results may vary markedly by using a different size egg than called for. For 4 medium eggs in a recipe substitute 3X large or 5 small.

size of your loaf. When baking in a pyrex pan, set heat 25 degrees lower. The top should be brown and the loaf should be crusty all round. It should sound dry and hollow when thumped and shouldn't be too soft if you squeeze the sides. You will learn by experience how to recognize a done loaf. Remove from pans immediately and let cool on wire racks.

## Ingredient Substitutions:

Whey for skim milk powder (SMP) – Heat whey enough to melt fat – omit SMP.

Non-instant SMP for Instant SMP. Decrease amount to ½ cup.

Molasses or honey or white sugar for brown sugar in equal amounts.

Margarine or butter or oil or other fat for lard.

Other flour mixtures for different effects. One cup of soy flour for one cup of whole wheat flour, gives a very moist well keeping loaf.

For 100% whole wheat bread – omit white flour. Loaf will be more compact.

*Variations:*

When you are at the loaf-making stage, part or all of the dough can be used as below:

1. Buns – Pinch off small pieces of dough. Bring rough edges to the bottom. Put into greased muffin tins or on cookie sheet. Proceed as above. Brush hot buns with fat if desired.

2. Sticky buns – Spread the bottom of an 8 inch square pan generously with butter or margarine and sprinkle generously with brown sugar. Toss on a handful of nuts. Take one of the portions of dough that you divided for loaves. Roll it out with a rolling pin or bottle to about ½ inch thickness. Spread top with soft butter or margarine. Sprinkle with a handful of brown sugar and a bit of cinnamon. Roll up. Cut roll into 1 inch slices. Place in pan and let rise thoroughly. Bake at 400 degrees F. for approximately 25 minutes. Turn out of pan immediately onto wire rack or plate.

3. Pizza crust – Roll out a small portion of dough as thin as piecrust (⅛ inch.) Put on oiled pizza pan or pie pan and trim; or press it to fit the pan with your hands or freeze for later use. Allow to puff slightly and prepare pizza.

4. Bread sticks – Roll small lumps of dough into pencil size rolls. Brush with egg whites and roll in sesame seeds. Let rise and bake until lightly browned. Don't burn the seeds.

5. Make a sponge – Follow the above recipe down to the place of adding the whole wheat flour but omit the salt. The mixture should be as thick as cake batter. Let it rise 1½ to 2 hours, sprinkle the salt over the surface of the risen sponge and stir, then continue as usual. (Salt inhibits the growth of yeast, so when you want to attain maximum growth, leave it out.)

# RYE BREAD
## Yield: 4 medium loaves

(All dry measures rounded for speed in mixing)
Sprinkle

**2 tsp yeast**

On

**½ cup lukewarm water**
**1 tsp sugar**

Stir and set aside.
Put into large bowl

**2 cups hot water**
**4 tbs fat (shortening, butter, margarine, or oil)**
**2 tbs honey**
**1 tsp anise seed or grated rind of one orange**
**2 eggs**
**½ cup molasses**
**2 cups white flour**
**2 cups whole wheat flour**

Test for heat on wrist. If lukewarm, add yeast mixture. Beat. Set in warm (85 degrees F.) moist place 2 hours or until risen and bubbly. Sprinkle over surface

**2 tsp salt**

Stir in

**Rye flour to make a stiff dough (about 4 cups)**

Turn out on floured board. Scrape bowl. Knead vigorously 10 to 20 minutes. Return to bowl. Set in warm moist place. (If rising place is not moist, cover bowl with clean damp cloth.) Let rise 2 hours or until double in bulk. Form into loaves. Place on greased cookie sheet or in greased bread pans. Let rise 2 hours or until light and high. Place in hot oven (400 degrees F.) After 10 minutes reset oven at 325 degrees. Bake bread 1 hour or until browned and crusty all around and hollow sounding when thumped. Cool on wire rack.

# ONION WHEELS
## Yield: 16 large or 32 small wheels

Really fantastic with spaghetti. A good crisp bread for any spread. Terrific for travelling.
Sprinkle

**1 tsp sugar (round it up)**
**1 tsp yeast**

Into

**½ cup lukewarm water**

Stir and set aside.

Heat in large pan

> **6 tbs oil**

Sauté gently until soft but not brown

> **3 cups fine chopped onions**

Add

> **½ cup cold water**
> **1 tsp salt**

When mixture is lukewarm add

> **yeast mixture** and **about 4 cups flour***

Make a firm dough.

Turn out on floured board and knead 10 to 20 minutes. Let rise as directed on page 61. Punch down. Form into 16 or 32 balls. Let rest in warm moist place or covered at room temperature for a few minutes. Roll or pat each ball into thin circle. (This is the hard part. It is worth your time to pause and figure out how you can best get these stretchy little balls into thin circles. My best success is in pressing them with the heel of my hand directly on greased cookie sheets. The end product should be mainly crispy. To accomplish this you must get them quite thin.) Place on greased cookie sheets and let rise 1½ hours or until light. Bake at 350 degrees F. 20 minutes or until golden brown top and bottom. If bottom rack wheels are browning faster than those on top or vice versa, switch position of pans half way through baking.

*Variations:*

Omit onions
Add cheese before flour.
Press seeds or cooked chick peas into wheels.
Brush tops with oil.
Bake on oven racks instead of pans.
Fry instead of baking. The Russians fry these in a small amount of fat until brown on both sides.
Leave out yeast, and put directly in oven after mixing ingredients and rolling thin.

## BOSTON BROWN BREAD
### Yield: 3 small loaves

Good with margarine or cheese spread as part of a meal or snack.
Set oven at 275 degrees F.
Sift together or mix carefully

> **1 cup rye flour**
> **1 cup yellow cornmeal**

---

\* See Cooking Note #2 page 58.

**1 cup whole wheat flour**
**1½ tsp baking soda**
**1 tsp salt**

Add

**¾ cup molasses**
**2 cups sour milk**
**1 cup raisins**

Mix. Pour into small greased loaf pans and bake 1½ hours or until inserted tooth pick comes out clean.

To Steam – Pour batter into well greased molds. Fill each mold ⅔ full. Tie a greased cover on with string. Place molds on a platform in a large pot. Fill pot with boiling water to half way up the mold. Cover. Simmer for 3½ hours. Add more boiling water as needed.

Note – Sweet milk or water may be substituted for sour milk. Decrease amount to 1¾ cups. Dates may be substituted for raisins.


## HOT BISCUITS
### Yield: 12 biscuits

Set oven at 450 degrees F.
Measure into sifter

**2 cups sifted flour***
**½ tsp salt**
**½ tsp baking soda****
**2 tsp baking powder**

Sift. If using whole wheat flour add back any bran that is left in sifter.
Cut in or rub in

**¼ cup fat**

Make a little well in center of mixture. Add all at once

**¾ cup buttermilk or ⅔ cup whey**

Mix round and round with a few strokes of a spoon. Turn out onto a floured board. Gather into a soft ball. Pat here and there with a bit of flour if sticky. Pat or roll to ½ inch thickness. Cut out with 2 inch or 3 inch cookie cutter. Place on greased or ungreased cookie sheet. Bake 10 minutes or until brown.

You will get the nicest biscuits from a quite soft dough though it

---

* If you do not sift flour before measuring, decrease quantity by one tablespoon per cup.
** See Cooking Note #3 page 59.

is a bit hard to manage. The old country way of baking biscuits is to melt 2 to 3 tbs fat on the cookie sheet and turn each biscuit over greasing top and bottom, to make a crispy savory crust. There is modern prejudice against such a practice, but it's the total fat content of your diet that counts. If you want to put part of your moderate fat intake on top of your biscuits because it tastes good, do so with pleasure. For proper results these biscuits should be made quickly and baked immediately in a very hot oven.

# MUFFINS
## Yield: 12 medium muffins

Set oven at 400 degrees F.
Grease 12 muffin tins lightly.
Sift together

> **1¾ cup whole wheat flour**
> **½ tsp salt**
> **3 tsp baking powder**

Mix in

> **3 to 4 tbs sugar**

Mix

> **1 slightly beaten egg**
> **1 cup milk**
> **¼ cup melted fat or oil**

Add all at once to flour mixture. Combine with 12 strokes of the spoon. Over-mixing toughens muffins. Spoon into muffin tins. Bake 10 minutes or until browned.

*Variations:*

1. Light muffins – substitute ¾ cup cake and pastry flour for ¾ cup whole wheat flour.
2. Fruit muffins – add ½ cup raisins, chopped dates or figs with the liquid ingredients.
3. Apple muffins – sift ½ tsp cinnamon with the dry ingredients. Add ½ cup grated raw apple with the liquid ingredients.
4. Cheese muffins – decrease sugar to 2 tbs. Add ½ cup grated cheese to dry ingredients. Increase milk to 1¼ cups.
5. Molasses muffins – decrease sugar to 1 tbs and baking powder to 2 tsp. Sift ¼ tsp baking soda with dry ingredients. Add 3 tbs molasses to liquid ingredients.
6. Buttermilk muffins – decrease baking powder to 2 tsp. Sift ½ tsp baking soda with dry ingredients. Substitute buttermilk, yogurt or whey for milk.

## RYE CRACKERS
### Yield: 20 small Crackers

Set oven at 375 degrees F.
Combine and mix until smooth

> 1 cup rye flour
> ¾ cup whole wheat flour
> 1 tsp baking powder
> 1 tsp sugar
> ¼ tsp salt
> 1 to 2 tsp cumin seed
> ½ cup melted margarine
> ½ cup milk

Divide into 2 balls. Chill for easier handling if you wish. Roll thin. Cut into diamonds. Prick with a fork. Bake 10 minutes or until just beginning to brown. Cool thoroughly. Store in airtight tin.

## SESAME CRACKERS
### Yield: 3 dozen small Crackers

A snap to make!
Set oven at 350 degrees F.
Mix in a bowl

> 1½ cup wholewheat flour
> ¼ cup soy flour
> ¼ cup sesame seeds
> ¾ tsp salt

Sprinkle over dry ingredients

> ¼ cup oil

Blend well with spoon or fingers. Add

> ½ cup water

Mix. Form into a ball. Roll out to ⅛ inch. Cut in squares. Prick with fork. Place on cookie sheet. Bake 15 minutes or until faint browning appears. Crackers should be done through, but not over-brown. Cool thoroughly. Store in airtight tin.

## SCOTTISH OATCAKES
### Yield: 12 – 4 inch Cakes

Set oven at 375 degrees F.
Mix in large bowl

> 3 cups quick oats*

---

\* If you use large flake or old fashioned rolled oats whirl them in a blender or chop them up a bit.

1 tsp salt
1 tsp baking powder

Pour over all

½ cup melted lard

Mix thoroughly.
Add

½ cup hot water
¼ cup whole wheat flour or enough to make a soft dough

Form into a ball. Press ball flat. Roll thin. Cut out with 4 inch
cookie cutter. Score with a cross in the center. Bake 15 minutes or
until the faintest bit of brown begins to show around the edges. Cool
thoroughly. Store in airtight tin.

Note – Some people add 1 tbs sugar to the above.

## DATE LOAF
### Yield: 1 – 5 x 11 inch Loaf

Set oven at 325 degrees F.
Mix

1 cup boiling water
1 cup chopped dates
1 tbs margarine or other shortening

Cover and let stand. Beat together

1 egg
1 cup demerara sugar

Combine with date mixture.
Sift together

1¾ cup sifted whole wheat flour
¼ tsp salt
¼ tsp baking soda
2 tsp baking powder

Add back any bran left in the sifter. Combine flour mixture with
date mixture.
Add

½ cup chopped nuts (if desired)

Pour into greased loaf pan. Bake 1¼ hours or until loaf shrinks
slightly from sides of pan and tooth pick or cake tester comes out
clean.

## BANANA BREAD
### Yield: 1 – 5 x 11 Inch Loaf

This is especially good with real stone ground flour.
Set oven at 350 degrees F.
Cream together

**½ cup margarine** (or butter if it is available)
**½ cup demerara sugar**

Add

**2 well beaten eggs**
**1 cup mashed bananas**
**1 tsp lemon juice**

Sift together

**2 cups sifted flour**
**3 tsp baking powder**
**¼ tsp salt**

Add back any bran left in the sifter. Combine quickly with banana mixture.
Add

**1 cup chopped nuts**

Put batter into greased loaf pan. Bake 1 hour or until loaf shrinks slightly from sides of pan and tooth pick or cake tester comes out clean.


## SOUPS

For a super happy family get into the soup-making habit. It is a beautiful way to get good use from all those little bits of things that generally get thrown away, including nutritious vegetable water.

Wash all your vegetables before you put them away. Then when you core a cabbage or a green pepper or cut the leaves and end off a head of celery put them into a little plastic bag in your freezer or ice cube compartment to wait for the next pot of soup. If you cook and drain a vegetable save the juice and start a pot of soup right away.

It's kind of fun testing recipes at home. What I lose in scientific precision I make up in intensity and authenticity of experience.

Husband, Jerry, walks through the house with his coat on – just stopped to pick up the mail on his way to a meeting down town.

"Would you like a bowl of soup?" I asked.

"No," he says, "have barely enough time to make my meeting."

"Too bad. It's good soup. Maybe you could take some in a cup."

I set a cupful of "Dutch Bean Soup" down on a counter and continued putting food out for children who had filled up the kitchen. Ten minutes later I noticed Jerry standing beside the soup kettle serving himself another cupful. He didn't have to fill out a weighted questionnaire to inform me of his evaluation. If the soup was worth making the Mayor and all the Councillors wait, it was *good soup*.

I used to make soup with small success. Three events changed me into a super souper.

One day I was cleaning out the refrigerator to make soup. I did it every week or two. "This for the soup, this for the garbage, this for the soup, this for the fridge again." It suddenly dawned on me, "You'll never get anywhere unless you decide where you're going. If you're going to make soup, consider the soup; if you're going to empty the refrigerator, call it house cleaning and shed no tears."

I was making soup when my Polish neighbour, Mary Gambol, walked in.

"You can always make good soup if you remember four things," she said. She hadn't knocked or said, "Hello."

I looked up . . . stunned, I guess.

"Parsley, garlic, onion, and celery," she said.

I never forgot it. *Parsley, garlic, onion, celery.* It's easy to remember. And it's true you can always make good soup if you season your stock with those four friendly foods. Vary your seasoning of course. Change them altogether – sure. But you can't beat it for a stand-by.

My third step to better soup came when I admitted I was sipping good soup, but chewing lousy vegetables. The vegetables you use to season the stock must be discarded. By the time the soup is done, the original onion has become limp and brown. It has given its life for the soup. Give it a dignified memorial service and toss it out. I have discovered one hedge. After 1 hour the vegetables are still edible. If you start your dinner soup at 11:00 a.m., at 12:00 you can remove the seasoning vegetables and have them for lunch with bread and butter. Then finish cooking the soup for dinner.

# COUNTRY POTATO SOUP
## Yield: 4½ Cups

Simple and good.
Heat in a large pot to boiling

**2 cups water (or enough to almost cover potato slices)**

Add

**3 cups thin potato slices**
**¾ cup thin onion slices**
**1 tsp dried parsley**

Return liquid to a boil. Reduce heat. Simmer 10 minutes or until vegetables are tender.
Mix (in cup or bowl)

**1 cup milk**
**1 tbs flour**
**1 tbs margarine**
**1 tsp salt**
**Generous dash black pepper**

Pour into simmering potatoes gently lifting them off the bottom so the milk can run underneath. Agitate the soup so that the milk heats evenly and doesn't lump but not so much that you break the potato slices. Return to boiling point. Remove from heat. Serve immediately. Small amounts of other vegetables such as fine chopped green peppers, celery or cabbage may be cooked with the potatoes for variation. If you are having a feast, you can add a small tin of tiny shrimps.

# GREEK POTATO SOUP
## Yield: 6 Cups

Just a little bother gives you a very elite soup. A soup to remember.
Heat in heavy pan

**2 tbs margarine**

Sauté* until soft but not brown

**½ cup chopped onions**

Add and stir until bubbly

**2 tbs flour**

Add and mix

**4 cups soup stock (chicken stock preferred)**
**2 cups sliced potatoes**
**½ tsp salt**

---

* To sauté cook over medium heat turning with spatula, egg turner or spoon to insure even browning.

72

Bring to a boil. Simmer 30 minutes. Rub soup through a sieve. Taste carefully. Add salt if required. Reduce heat. (Perfect flavour in this soup is dependent on exactly the right amount of salt.)
Beat in cup or bowl with a whisk

**2 egg yolks**

Add gradually, beating

**1 cup milk**
**1 cup hot soup**

Add to hot but not boiling soup beating vigorously with a whisk. The Greeks prefer their soup not quite so hot as we North Americans take it. (If you boil this soup it will curdle, spoiling the creamy appearance and smooth taste although not the flavour.) Garnish with snipped chives or parsley or with a slice of lemon. For variation beat 2 tbs lemon juice into the egg yolks before adding the milk.

## FRENCH ONION SOUP

### Yield: 5 Cups

"Why don't we have onion soup?" asked my 5 year old son.
   "It's too expensive," I replied.
   "Are onions expensive?" he asked.
The implications of Eddy's gentle query were obvious. I made onion soup for the first time that day. Eddy liked it so much that he learned to make it too. He's 17 now and the family onion soupmaker. He has the patience to stand and stir the onions in the butter or margarine until they caramelize a bit. They turn a rich brown and give off a most compelling aroma.

Heat in a heavy pan

**2 tbs butter or margarine**

Add and sauté over medium heat until dark brown (don't burn them)

**2½ cups sliced onions**

Add

**4 cups soup stock\***

Bring to a boil. Simmer gently for 5 minutes.
Pour soup over

**Thick slices of whole wheat bread**

Sprinkle with

**Grated Parmesan Cheese**

---

\* I like to use Oxo cubes to make the stock for this soup although any well flavoured soup stock should be satisfactory. A spoonful of miso paste, a savory paste made from soy beans, found in Chinese groceries, should be added to your vegetable stock to give it a rich colour and hearty taste.

# RUTABAGA SOUP
## Yield: 4 Servings

Heat in saucepan

**2 tbs margarine**

Sauté

**¼ cup chopped green onions** (or dry onions)

Add

**2 cups coarsely grated rutabaga turnip**
**1 cup boiling water**

Return to a boil. Reduce heat. Simmer 10 minutes or until turnip is tender.

Add

**3 cups milk**
**1½ tbs flour**
**1 tsp salt**
**⅛ tsp pepper**
**generous grating nutmeg***

Swish with fork or whisk to break up any flour lumps. Return to boiling over medium heat. Serve with tasty crackers or wholewheat bread and butter.


# LENTIL SOUP, INDIAN STYLE
## Yield: 5 Cups

Heat to boiling in a large pot

**6 cups water**

Add

**1 cup washed whole or split lentils**

Return to boil. Reduce heat. Simmer until lentils are tender (about 30 minutes for split lentils; 1½ hours for whole lentils.) Mash.
Heat in heavy pan

**2 tbs oil**

Sauté until brown around the edges

**1 slivered onion****

---

\* For a lovely haunting flavour buy the whole nutmegs and grate a little as you need it.

\*\* A bachelor cut onion. Cut pieces off the onion so they are thick in the middle, thin on the edges.

Add

    **2 tsp salt**
    **¼ tsp chili powder**
    **1 tsp ground turmeric**
    **½ tsp ground cumin**
    **1 tsp ground coriander**

Sauté 1 minute or until the spices smell cooked. (Do not burn!) Add to lentils – If soup is too thick add a little water.
Add

    **1 tbs margarine**

Return to boil. Reduce heat. Simmer 30 minutes or until flavours are well blended.

## SUNNY BEAN SOUP
### Yield: 5 Cups

Wash and place in large pot
**1 cup whole dry white, navy, red, or lima beans, or lentils**
Add

    **5 cups water**

Soak overnight.
Chop

    **1 onion**
    **1 celery branch**
    **1 carrot**
    **1 garlic clove**

Sauté in

    **4 tbs hot oil**

Add

    **2 tbs tomato paste**
    **1 tsp parsley flakes** (or more fresh parsley)
    **1 bay leaf**

Add to beans or lentils. Bring to boil. Reduce heat. Simmer until *nearly* tender.
Add

    **1 tsp salt**

Continue simmering until beans or lentils are tender.
Add

    **1 tbs vinegar**

Serve hot. If you prefer a thicker soup, make a paste of 3 tbs flour and ½ cup cooled soup and add with the salt. Or, for variation add ¼ tsp oregano and ¼ cup cooked tomatoes when adding salt.

# DUTCH BEAN SOUP
## Yield: 4 Cups

This is a scrumptious bean soup and uniquely flexible.
Wash, pick over, and place in cooking pot

**1 cup dry beans (pinto, navy, or lima)**

Add

**6 cups water**

Soak over night.
Add

**1 tsp salt**
**3 whole cloves**
**6 peppercorns**
**1 bayleaf**

Bring to boil. Reduce heat. Simmer 2 hours. Rub through sieve.
Heat in heavy pan

**2 tbs fat**

Sauté

**⅓ cup slices celery and leaves**
**⅓ cup slices or shredded carrots**

Add to soup. Thin with boiling water if necessary. Return to boil.
Reduce heat. Simmer 20 minutes or until flavours mix.
Add

**1½ tbs soy sauce**
**1½ tbs catsup**

*Variations:*

1. If you are out of celery, try using ⅓ cup slivered onion and ¼ tsp oregano.
2. If you like a creamy bean soup add ⅓ cup evaporated milk at the end. The soup is good enough to eat before adding the carrots and celery or immediately thereafter when the vegetables are still a bit crunchy.
3. Curry Soup – Heat 3 cups of Dutch bean soup, (thinned with water if necessary). Sauté 2 chopped onions in a little oil, and add 1½ tbs of flour and 1½ tsp of curry powder to them. Brown the mixture a little, add enough soup to mix, then return the onion mixture to the pot of soup. Bring to a boil and simmer 10 minutes.

For my bachelor friend, I recommend Dutch Bean Soup.

Sunday night: Wash 2 cups (double recipe) of beans and soak overnight as above.

Monday morning: Season and simmer while getting ready for work.

Monday night: Continue cooking beans until tender. Have a hearty meal of beans, bread and butter and a salad.

Tuesday night: Run beans through a sieve or mash them. Sauté vegetables as directed. Mix with pureed beans. Simmer and eat a savoury bean soup with chunks of oven toasted bread, a couple of olives, and a slice of good cheese.

Wednesday night: Simmer soup. (Add water when necessary.) Season with catsup and soy sauce. Eat along with a bowl of rice and bean sprouts.

Thursday night: Heat soup. Thin with cream or evaporated milk. Toss on some crispy croutons.

Friday night: Use the left over soup (if you should be so lucky) to make Curry Soup (page 76, variation 3.)

There you are, bachelor friend . . . cheap, nourishing, delicious, small labour input, interesting and satisfying.

# BEAN AND BARLEY SOUP
## Yield: 7 cups

A very mild flavoured pleasant soup.
Rinse and pick over

> **1 cup dry lima beans**

Place in pot.
Add

> **6 cups cold water**
> **2 tsp salt**
> **¼ tsp pepper**

Cover. Bring to boil. Reduce heat. Simmer 1½ hours.
Add

> **¼ cup minced onion**
> **½ cup diced carrot**
> **3 tbs pot barley**

Bring to boil. Reduce heat. Simmer 1½ hours.
Add

> **1 cup evaporated milk**
> **2 tbs butter or margarine**
> **2 tbs parsley**

Bring to boiling point. Serve.


# PEA SOUP
## Yield: 3-4 Cups

Wash and pick over

> **1 cup dry split peas**

Soak overnight in

> **3 cups water**

Add

> **1 tbs bacon bits** (natural or soy produce)
> **¼ tsp celery seed**
> **1 bay leaf**
> **1 tsp parsley flakes** (fresh preferred)
> **1 tsp salt**
> **Dash pepper**
> **¼ tsp thyme** (if desired)

Simmer 1 hour or until peas are soft. For extra smoothness, rub through a sieve. Dilute with

> **1 cup milk** (more or less depending on thickness desired)

Serve with whole wheat toast on a cold day.

## MISO SOUP
### Yield: 5 Cups

Heat in a heavy pan

**2 tbs oil**

Sauté 5 minutes

**1 cup slivered onions**
**2 cups sliced cabbage**
**1 cup carrots, sliced diagonally**

Add to

**5 cups boiling water**

Bring to boil. Reduce heat. Simmer 30 minutes or until vegetables are tender.
Beat together in a small bowl

**3 heaping tbs Miso paste** (see page 73 footnote)
**½ cup water**

Add to soup. Bring to boil. Reduce heat. Simmer 10 minutes.
Garnish with

**Chopped green onions**


## MINESTRONE SOUP
### Yield: 5 Cups

Wash and pick over

**1 cup dry white beans**

Soak overnight in

**4 cups water**

Add

**1 clove garlic**
**1 onion**
**2 tsp parsley flakes**
**1 stalk celery or ½ tsp celery seeds**

Bring to a boil. Reduce heat. Simmer 2 hours or until beans are tender. Remove 2 cups of cooked beans and reserve for another purpose. (One cup beans and a tasty stock should remain in pot.)
Add

**2 tsp salt**
**1 diced carrot**

**1 tbs green pepper**
**1 cup coarsely shredded cabbage**
**1 cup tomatoes**
**2 tbs tomato paste**
**½ tsp oregano**
**Water if needed**

Bring to boil. Reduce heat. Simmer 20 minutes or until vegetables are tender.
Add

**1 cup cooked Spaghetti**

Heat and serve with large chunks of whole wheat or rye bread.

## GAZPACHO ANDALUZ
### Yield: 4 servings

Gazpacho and dark bread is the traditional lunch taken out to the field for the farm workers of Andalusia.
Chop fine:

**2 ripe tomatoes**
**⅓ large cucumber**
**½ red or green sweet pepper**
**½ sweet onion** or **4 green onions** (the white and part of the green)

Put into large bowl in cool place.
Pulverize in a large mortar (or heavy bowl with a wooden masher)

**1 – 1½ cloves garlic**

Add and keep pulverizing

**½ tsp salt**
**¼ tsp pepper**
**½ cup fine dry breadcrumbs**

Add, 1 teaspoon at a time, and keep pulverizing

**3 tbs oil** (olive oil, if available)
**2 tsp white vinegar**

Add more quickly

**½ cup cold water**

Pour this sauce over the chopped vegetables. Mix gently.
Lay over top

**½ pound small ice cubes**

(Put 1 cup water into a 2 cup measure. Add enough ice cubes to bring the water level up to the 2 cup line. Quickly drain off the water and you have ½ lb ice left.) Set Gazpacho back in cool place until ready to serve. Remove any remaining ice pieces and stir before serving. This is the traditional method for Gazpacho. You may use a blender to speed things up, but make sure everything is thoroughly pulverized and thoroughly mixed. The result is a very unique and beautiful flavour.

## YOGURT SOUP
### Yield: 5 cups

Very refreshing. Leaves the most beautiful feeling in your tummy.
Grind in a mortar

> **3 tbs chopped walnuts**
> **½ tsp salt**
> **1 clove garlic**
> **Dash pepper**

Add gradually and grind

> **4 tbs olive oil**
> **1 tbs vinegar**

Transfer to large bowl.
Add

> **½ cup ice water**
> **3½ cups yogurt**
> **1 cup chopped peeled cucumber**

Add

> **More ice water** if too thick

Serve very cold. Buttermilk can be substituted for yogurt but omit the ice water.

## GRAINS

### STEAMED GRAINS

We are used to eating rice as a main dish or part of a main dish. Buckwheat, Barley, Millet, Cracked Wheat can be cooked and eaten in basically the same ways.

| Bring to boil | Add ½ tsp salt and | Simmer |
|---|---|---|
| 2¼ cups water | 1 cup brown rice | 30 minutes* |
| 3 cups water | 1 cup millet | 30 minutes |
| 2 cups water | 1 cup whole buckwheat | 30 minutes |
| 2½ cups water | 1 cup cracked wheat | 45 minutes |
| 3 cups water | 1 cup pot barley | 1½ hours |
| 3 cups water | 1 cup wheat kernels | 2 hours |

* Or until the grain is as tender as you like it.

Serve steamed grains with butter or a dollop of yogurt, with your favourite sauce, or in a savoury casserole.

NOTE – For best results cook in a pot with a tightly fitting cover.

## RICES, CURRIES, VARIETY AND EGG DISHES

Rice and other whole grains are mild and pleasantly flavoured – basically nourishing, cheap. If you have taken the vow of simplicity, you may have your bowl of whole grain, your whole milk curds, your cabbage leaf unadorned. If you like to live high while living cheap, take some cooking tips from the Chinese, the Ukranians, the East Indians on how to turn that simple meal into a feast.

### PARSLEY RICE
#### Yield: 4 Servings

This is lovely.
Set oven at 350 Degrees F.
Mix

> **2 cups cooked rice**
> **1 medium chopped onion**
> **1 cup chopped parsley** (fresh, or flakes soaked in water)
> **1½ cup grated cheese**
> **½ tsp salt**
> **1 cup milk**
> **2 beaten eggs**
> **½ cup oil**

Turn into a baking dish. Cover. Bake 1 hour.

### BARLEY CASSEROLE
#### Yield: 4 Servings

Steamed barley has a very mild, slightly sweet, fragrant taste. When constructing a barley based entrée, choose accompanying ingredients with bright definite flavour.
Set oven at 350 degrees F.
Heat in heavy pan

> **2 tbs oil**

Sauté until lightly brown

> **⅓ lb sliced mushrooms**
> **⅓ cup chopped green onions**
> **1 tbs sesame seeds**

Add

> **3 cups steamed barley (see page 81)**
> **1 tsp Worcestershire sauce**
> **⅓ cup grated parmesan cheese**
> **½ tsp paprika**
> **1 to 1½\* cups medium white sauce (see page 95)**

Mix and pour into casserole dish.
Top with

> **⅓ cup grated parmesan cheese**

Cover and bake 30 minutes or until heated through.

## CURRIES

My first curry was made by two young men who had grown up in India. They served the fiery stuff on mounds of rice and passed around little dishes of accompaniments they called "toley moleys." There should be something mild, something hot, something salty, something sweet. Each person can mix these to his own liking with his curry. If you put the toley moleys around your plate in daubs, mixing in a little of this, a little of that as you eat, each bite of curry can be a completely new taste.

## TOLEY MOLEYS

Toasted nuts
Sieved or chopped hard cooked egg
Chutney
Lemon pickle (from Indian specialty shops)
Raisins
Toasted coconut
Bacon bits (natural or soy product)
Chopped tomatoes, onions or green peppers
Sliced apples or bananas in yogurt (this is especially cooling to eat with very spicy curry).

## VEGETABLE CURRY
### Yield: 4 servings

This is an easy-to-make mild flavoured curry.
Heat in heavy pan

> **2 tbs ghee\*\*or oil**

---

\* If a Creamier Caserole is desired use 1½ cups white sauce.

\*\* Ghee is clarified butter or butter oil. It is preferred to fresh butter in hot countries because it has a longer shelf life. It doesn't burn as easily as ordinary butter. If you want to get some butter flavour into your curry, mix half butter and half oil.

Sauté until translucent*

**1½ cups onions**
**2 large cloves garlic**

Add and stir

**¾ tsp curry powder**

Add

**1 chopped egg plant** or **2 unpeeled zucchinis** or **1 pound green pumpkin**
**1 cup water or juice from firm canned tomatoes**
**4 medium tomatoes peeled and squashed**
**1 tsp salt**

Bring to boil. Reduce heat. Simmer 20 minutes or until vegetables are tender and flavours are blended.


## CURRIED EGGS, MADRASI STYLE

May be served along with curry or to add flavour and colour to an ordinary meal.

Peel and slice in half

**10 hard cooked eggs**

Heat in heavy pan

**3 tbs oil**

Sauté until brown around the edges

**½ cup slivered onions**

Remove to small dish.
Add to hot pan

**1 tsp mustard seeds**
**½ inch piece dry red chili**

Sauté until seeds pop and begin to smell cooked.
Add

**½ tsp turmeric**
**½ tsp paprika**
**½ tsp ground cloves**
**½ tsp ground ginger**
**1 tsp curry powder**
**¼ tsp garlic powder**
**½ tsp salt**

---

\* Until light shines through.

Sauté 30 seconds or until raw smell is gone from the spices. Don't burn anything. Carefully add the egg halves and the sautéed onions. Turn eggs to coat them with the spices on all sides. Sauté until eggs are slightly browned. Serve on small plate or as a garnish for a large platter of curry.

## MADRASI DAL
### Yield: ½ Cups

Bring to boil in cooking pot

Dal
- 2 cups water
- 1 cup split lentils
- 1½ tsp turmeric
- 2 tsp garlic powder
- 2 tsp ginger
- 1 chopped large tomato
- 2 small onions
- ¾ tsp salt

Reduce heat. Simmer 30 minutes or until lentils are soft. Mash dal. Set aside. Heat in heavy pan

**2 tbs oil**

Sauté until brown around the edges

**1 medium slivered onion**

Add and brown

**1 tsp mustard seed**

Add and brown

**3 or 4 dry red chilis**

Add mashed dal. Stir and heat. Serve with curry or steamed grains and vegetables.

No! I'm not kidding. These are the measured amounts of spices used to make this dal. Remember it is eaten in small amounts along with other foods. If you wish to be conservative try ½ tsp each turmeric, garlic powder and ginger, and only 1 red chili leaving the other ingredients as they are.

## CHANA DAL
### Yield: 6 Servings

Heat to boiling in cooking pot

**1 cup Chana Dal\* or substitute dry chick peas, lentils or split peas**

---

\* Chana Dal can be obtained in Indian groceries

> **5 cups cold water**
> **1 tsp salt**
> **1 heaping tsp mango powder** (or substitute 1 tbs lemon juice)

Reduce heat. Simmer 3 hours or until dal turns to mush.
Heat in heavy pan

> **4 tbs ghee** (or oil)

Sauté until crisp and brown around the edges

> **1¼ cup chopped onions**

Add

> **1 heaping tsp curry powder**
> **⅛ tsp fenugreek seeds** (if you have them)
> **¼ tsp black mustard seed** (or ordinary mustard seed)

Sauté 1 minute or until seeds pop. Don't burn them. Add to the dal. Add a bit of water if dal is very thick. Stir and cook 10 minutes or until flavours mix and dal is hot and of a good consistency. Serve with curry or vegetables and steamed grains.


# CHUTNEY
## Yield: 5 Cups

A delicious side dish for Indian foods.
Mix in saucepan

> **1 cup brown sugar**
> **1½ tsp salt**
> **½ tsp pepper**
> **½ tsp cinnamon**
> **½ tsp chili powder**

Add and mix

> **1 cup vinegar**
> **¼ cup molasses**

Add

> **3 cups chopped tomatoes**
> **1½ cups chopped apples**
> **½ cup raisins**
> **1 cup chopped dried figs**

Bring to boil. Reduce heat. Simmer 1 hour or until fruits are tender, flavours are mixed, and sauce is of the right consistency. If it becomes too dry, add a little water. Store in a jar with a good lid in refrigerator. Serve with curry or as a relish with any meal that needs added zip.

# HOLUBTCHI
## Yield: 6 generous servings

This is the cabbage roll that brought 2 generations of Ukrainians through hard times and good times on the prairies. They can still be had at weddings and reunions or made for you by a wise old baba.
Heat to boiling

**2 cups water**

Add

**2 cups rice**
**2 tsp salt**

Return to boil. Cook 1 minute. Cover tightly. Turn off heat. Let stand on hot burner until water is absorbed. (Rice will be only partially cooked.)
Heat in heavy pan

**4 tbs butter** or **pork dripping**

Sauté until translucent

**¾ cup finely chopped onion**

Mix with rice.
Add

**½ tsp paprika**
**Generous dash pepper**

This filling for cabbage rolls should be well seasoned as some of the flavour will be absored by the cabbage leaves. Cool.
Cut the core from

**1 large cabbage head**

Place cabbage in a large bowl. Pour boiling water into the hollow centre of the cabbage (enough to cover completely.)
Cover bowl and let stand until leaves are soft and pliable. Drain and take leaves apart carefully. Don't tear them. Trim the hard center rib from each leaf. Cut very large leaves into 2 or 3 sections. Line bottom of greased casserole with the cut off ribs and some outside or torn leaves. Place generous amount of rice filling on each leaf. Tuck in sides and roll lightly. Arrange rolls in layers. Lightly salt each layer.
Set oven at 350 degrees F.
Mix

**1½ cups tomato juice**
**½ cup yogurt**
**2 tbs melted fat**
**Salt and pepper to taste**

Pour over cabbage rolls. Lay a few large leaves over rolls. Cover casserole tightly. Bake 1 hour. Check cabbage rolls. If liquid is getting low, add a little water or tomato juice. Bake 30 minutes more or until cabbage and filling are cooked. Serve with Yogurt, sour cream or tomato sauce. Buckwheat can be substituted for the rice.

## SWISS QUICHE
### Cheese and Onion Pie
### Yield: one 9 inch pie

Set oven at 450 degrees F.
Heat in heavy skillet:

**2 tbs oil**

Add and toss about to coat with the fat

**3 or 4 thinly sliced medium onions**

Cover tightly. Steam over low heat until tender but not brown. Remove lid for last minute to evaporate any accumulated moisture. Beat in small bowl:

**2 eggs**
**2 egg yolks**
**1 cup milk**
**½ cup evaporated milk or cream**
**¾ tsp salt**
**½ tsp pepper**
**⅛ tsp nutmeg**
**1 cup Gruyère or sharp cheddar cheese**

Arrange onions evenly in

**1-9 inch unbaked pieshell**

Pour milk-egg-cheese mixture over onions. Bake 10 minutes. Reduce heat to 350 degrees F. and bake 20 minutes more or until quiche is set and puffy and a clean sharp knife blade comes out clean. Serve hot with a crispy salad.

## POMMES ET OEUFS
### Yield: 8 servings

A hearty supper dish. Set oven at 350 degrees

Bring to boil in large pot with good lid

**2 cups (more or less) water**

Peel quarter and add

**8 medium potatoes**

Return water to boiling. Reduce heat. Cook gently until tender. Drain, reserving cooking liquid for other purposes.

88

Add

    **¾ tsp salt (or to taste)**
    **⅛ tsp black pepper (or to taste)**
    **generous grating nutmeg**
    **2 tbs margarine**

Mash vigorously with wire masher or your favourite kind until all lumps have disappeared. Add in small amounts mashing vigorously after each addition until the potatoes are definitely light and fluffy.

    **¾ cup milk**

Pile into a baking dish. Make 8 indentations.
Add

    **8 fresh eggs**

Place one in each spot being careful not to break the yolks. Salt and pepper each egg.
On top of eggs lay gently

    **8 small slices sharp cheddar cheese**

Sprinkle over all

    **¼ cup bacon bits** (natural or soy product).

Bake 20 minutes or until eggs are set to your liking and cheese is melted. Serve with toast and a green salad.


## POACHED EGGS ITALIA
### Yield: 6 Servings

Heat in heavy pan

    **4 tbs oil (olive oil, if available)**

Sauté 2 minutes

    **1 minced clove garlic**
    **⅓ cup green onions**

Add

    **3 cups chopped tomatoes** (fresh or canned)
    **1 tbs chopped parsley**
    **dash cayenne**
    **¼ tsp salt**

Simmer over low flame about 25 minutes.
Carefully drop into sauce one at a time

    **6 fresh eggs**

Cover. Return to boil. Simmer 3 minutes. Serve on noodles or toast with a crispy salad.

## PASTAS AND SAUCES

A good pasta and a good sauce – always satisfying, always popular. Learn the knack and you can please any child, feed any crowd.

### WHOLE WHEAT NOODLES
### Yield: 1½ lbs

A tasty tender noodle that holds its shape well. Eat with butter or sauce. Use in casseroles or soups.

Beat together in large bowl

> **3 eggs**
> **1 cup lukewarm water**
> **1 tablespoon oil**
> **pinch salt**

Add, 1 cup at a time, beating after each addition

> **1 pound whole wheat flour**

When dough forms a ball, turn it onto a generously floured board. Knead vigorously 5 minutes, or until dough is smooth and elastic. Divide into 4 equal parts. Make a smooth ball of each part. Cover with a slightly damp cloth. Roll each ball into a very thin sheet, lifting dough and reflouring board as necessary to prevent sticking. Cut ¼ inch noodles from the dough by drawing sharp knife across entire surface or dust surface with flour, fold over 2 or 3 times, cut and unroll noodles.

For use the same day, dust with flour and refrigerate. If you wish to keep them longer spread noodles on racks or trays and leave in a warm dry place to dry out. The oven with the light on is a passable place. Leave the door open a little to allow for escape of moisture. To cook dried noodles, plunge into rapidly boiling, salted water and boil 10 minutes or until tender.

(Fresh noodles should require only 30 seconds in boiling water.) Cooking time will vary with thickness of noodles. The cooking water of these noodles is quite tasty and wholesome. Use for soup or cooking breakfast cereal.

### EASY POTLUCK CASSEROLE
### Yield: 4 Large Servings

Heat to boiling in large pot

> **4 cups water**
> **1 tsp salt**

Add

> **½ lb whole wheat noodles**

Stir. Return to boiling. Cook 10 minutes or until tender. Drain noodles.
Rinse with

**1 cup cold water**

Save liquid for other use.
Put into heavy skillet or cooking pot

**3½ cups (one 28 oz can) chopped tomatoes**
**½ cup chopped onion**
**½ cup chopped celery**
**1 tsp salt**
**1 tsp worcestershire sauce**
**½ tsp oregano**

Bring to a boil. Reduce heat, cook gently 20 minutes. Remove from heat. Add noodles and

**1 cup grated cheddar cheese**

Pour into buttered 1½ cup casserole. Sprinkle with more cheese.

Bake at 350 degrees 30 minutes.


## CREAMED CABBAGE AND NOODLES
### Yield: 4 Servings

Cook as directed opposite

**½ lb whole wheat noodles**

Heat in heavy skillet

**3 tbs margarine**

Add

**1 small (2 lb) thinly sliced cabbage head**

Toss cabbage around a bit to evenly coat it with fat. Lower heat, cover tightly, stir occasionally. Simmer 10 minutes or until cabbage is nearly tender. Sprinkle with

**2 tbs flour**
**1 tsp salt**
**¼ tsp pepper**
**⅛ tsp fresh grated nutmeg**
**1½ cups milk**

Mix. Heat until bubbly. Add noodles. Pour into a 1½ quart casserole dish. Top with

**1 cup buttered bread cubes**
**¼ cup grated parmesan cheese**

Bake in 350 degree oven 30 minutes or until bread cubes are brown and sauce is bubbly.

## BARRY'S KILLER LASAGNA
### Yield: 6 Generous Servings

Barry Archibald makes this for the Banyan Tree restaurant in Winnipeg.

Heat in heavy skillet

>   **2 tbs oil**

Sauté until translucent

>   **1 cup sliced onions**

Add and sauté 5 minutes

>   **½ cup diced carrots**
>   **½ cup diced celery**
>   **¼ tsp garlic powder**

Add and sauté 1 minute

>   **1½ tsp oregano**
>   **¼ tsp celery seed**
>   **1 tsp thyme**
>   **1½ tsp ground rosemary**
>   **1½ tsp basil**
>   **1 tsp chili powder**
>   **1½ tsp salt**

Stir in

>   **2 cups tomato paste**
>   **1 tbs honey**
>   **2 cups water**

Bring to a boil. Reduce heat. Simmer 1 hour. Cook according to package instructions

>   **20 lasagna noodles** or

make ¼ noodle recipe on page 90. Cover bottom of pan sparsely with sauce. Add a layer of noodles, cottage cheese, cheddar cheese and sauce. Repeat layers. End with mozzarella and a little sauce on top. Amounts of cheese to use are

**8 oz cheddar**
**8 oz mozzarella**
**1½ lb dry cottage cheese**

Bake at 300 degrees for 50 minutes or until lasagna is bubbling. Let cool 10 minutes. Serve with crisp salad.

## ITALIAN TOMATO SAUCE
### Yield: 2 Cups Sauce

This is a good basic tomato sauce. Use it with spaghetti, lasagna or beans.
Heat in heavy pan

**2 tbs oil**

Sauté until light brown

**½ cup chopped onions**
**1 minced clove garlic** (don't burn it!)
**½ inch whole dry red chili**

Add and sauté

**¾ cup tomato paste***

Add

**1 tsp salt**
**½ tsp sugar**
**1 tsp basil**
**1½ cups water**

Taste. If the sauce is too tart add

**½ tsp sugar**

Bring to boil. Reduce heat. Simmer 40 minutes. Occasionally give the sauce a real brisk stirring to keep it smooth. If sauce becomes too thick the emulsion breaks and the oil sits around in little pools. Add a bit of water as necessary to keep a smooth texture. Remove chili. Celery seed, parsley, green pepper, oregano may be used instead of, or in addition to the basil.

---

\* Tomato paste is thick unseasoned tomato pulp. If you use "tomato sauce" you must adjust for the water and seasonings contained therein. Left over tomato paste keeps well if you store it in a glass or plastic container. Cover it tightly and freeze or spread a thin film of oil over the surface and store in the refrigerator.

## GREEK STYLE TOMATO SAUCE
### Yield: 3 Cups

Heat in large heavy pan

**3 tbs oil** (olive oil if available)

Add one at a time and sauté until beginning to brown before adding the next

**1 cup chopped onions**
**1 tbs chopped garlic**
**½ inch whole dry red chili**
**1 tbs ground cinnamon**
**¾ cup tomato paste**

Stir in

**2 cups water**

Bring to boil. Reduce heat. Simmer 30 minutes or until flavours are mixed and sauce is of right consistency. If it becomes too thick add a little water. Serve with spaghetti or as a sauce for beans.


## SPAGHETTI AUX ROMAN EMPIRE
### Yield: 6 Servings

This is really good and a neat trick to know for that moment of emergency when the spaghetti sauce has run out and you still have a few people to feed.

Bring to boil in large pot

**6 quarts water**
**1 tbs salt**

Add

**1½ lb spaghetti noodles**

Boil 10 minutes.
While spaghetti is boiling assemble

**8 slightly beaten egg yolks (or 4 whole eggs)**
**½ cup bacon bits (natural or soy product)**
**½ cup grated parmesan cheese**
**2 tbs olive oil**
**½ tsp freshly ground pepper**

When spaghetti is tender but still slightly firm, drain and transfer immediately to a large heated oiled bowl. Add egg yolks. Toss. Add other assembled ingredients. Toss and serve immediately.

# MEDIUM WHITE SAUCE
## Yield: 1 cup

Learn to make a white sauce easily. You'll be forever glad you did.

Melt in saucepan

**2 tbs butter or margarine**

Stir in

**2 tbs flour**

Add gradually stirring

**1 cup milk**

Add

**½ tsp salt**
**Dash pepper**

Stir constantly over medium heat until thick and beginning to boil.
Lower heat and stir one more minute.

*Variations:*

Nearly all gravies and sauces are a variation of this recipe: Here are
only a few.

1. Thin Sauce – Add to cooked vegetables for cream soup.
   Decrease butter and flour to 1 tbs each.
2. Thick Sauce – For binding things together in loaves or patties.
   Increase butter and flour to 4 tbs each.
3. Cheese Sauce – Stir ½ cup grated cheese (aged cheese and process cheese melt best) into the sauce as it begins to boil. Use with
   macaroni, vegetables, in caseroles.
4. Mushroom or Onion Sauce – Sauté 1 cup sliced onions or mushrooms (fresh, frozen, soaked, dried, or drained canned) 3 minutes before adding flour or add cooked onions or mushrooms as
   the sauce begins to thicken. Eat on toast, with spaghetti, on vegetables, or in casseroles.
5. Egg Sauce – Fold in chopped hard cooked eggs.

## BEANS (LEGUMES)

Beans have been classed as poor man's food in our culture – always nourishing, always cheap, never much fun.

Beans can be beautiful! Cook them carefully. Keep them barely covered with water or sauce. Never let them dry out in the pan or in the refrigerator. Many beans have a very mild flavour. They lend themselves to light, bright seasoning as well as to hearty or pungent seasoning. To cook dry beans without soaking them overnight: wash them, cover them generously with water in a pot, heat to boiling, turn off heat, allow to sit for 1 hour, proceed according to recipe for soaked beans. In hot weather, beans soaking overnight should be kept in the refrigerator.

Most of the following recipes call for white beans or red beans. The recipes are mostly traditional ones developed in locales where particular beans were available. Use whatever beans you find at reasonable prices. Adjust the seasonings as necessary. Soy beans may be used in any of these recipes by increasing cooking time. They have about 50% more protein than many other beans and are reasonably priced higher. Soy beans at 60¢/lb are a better buy (protein-wise) than white beans at 45¢/lb.

## BASIC BEANS
### Yield: 3 Cups beans
### 2 Cups soup stock
### 1 cooked onion

Soak overnight

> 1 cup dry beans
> 4 cups water

When ready, bring to rapid boil. Boil 5 minutes. Skim off any solid matter that rises to the top.

Season with

> ¾ tsp salt
> 1 clove garlic
> 1 tsp parsley flakes
> 1 onion
> ¼ tsp celery seed
> **Vegetable parts** and other seasonings with discretion

Bring to a boil. Reduce heat. Simmer 1 hour or until beans are tender. Save the stock for soup or other dish. Eat beans hot with ketchup or Chinese oyster sauce, (available in Chinese grocery stores) or cold with chopped onions, olive oil, feta cheese and black olives or with pepper sauce. Use them in any recipe calling for cooked beans. Any kind of bean may be cooked in this way. Cooking time and yield of stock and beans will vary. Longer cooking time may require extra water. If you have no use for soup stock decrease water to 3 cups.

## BAR-B-QUED BEANS ON A BUN
### Yield: 7 Cups

A whole wheat bun if you please.

Soak overnight in large pot

**2 cups dry red beans**
**6 cups water**

Add

**¼ tsp ground ginger or cloves**

Bring to boil. Reduce heat. Simmer 1 hour or until beans begin to become tender.
Heat in heavy pot.

**2 tbs oil**

Sauté

**1 chopped onion**
**1 clove minced garlic**
**½ inch whole dry red chili**
**⅓ chopped sweet green pepper**
**1 tsp chili powder**
**¾ cup tomato paste**
**1 tbs brown sugar or honey**
**1 tsp salt**

Add liquid off beans to make a sauce. Pour the whole thing over the beans. Bring to boil. Reduce heat. Simmer 30 minutes or until the beans are tender, flavours are mixed, and sauce is just the right consistency. Add a bit of water if the sauce becomes too thick and the oil begins to separate. If the sauce is too thin boil rapidly for a few minutes stirring to prevent burning. Ladle over split buns.

# CHILI CON FRIJOLES
## Yield: 7 Cups

Soak overnight in cooking pot

**2 cups dry red beans**

in

**6 cups of water**

Next morning add

**¼ tsp cumin seed**

Bring to a boil and simmer gently 1½ hours or until nearly tender. Set aside.
Heat in heavy pot

**2 tbs oil**

Add one at a time. Sauté each a minute or two before adding the next

**1 chopped onion**
**1 garlic clove**
**½ inch piece dry red chili**
**½ tsp crushed cumin seed**
**2 tsp chili powder**
**¾ cup tomato paste**
**2 tsp salt**

Don't scorch anything. Gradually add the bean liquid stirring to make a sauce. Pour over the beans. Bring to a boil and simmer gently 20 minutes. If the sauce becomes too dry add a bit of water. The beans should be thoroughly tender and nearly covered with a rich bubbly sauce.


# HUEVOS RANCHEROS
## Yield: 6 Servings

A feast.

Mash or force through a sieve

**2 cups cooked red beans**

Add

**Salt and pepper to taste**

Mix

**3 cups cooked salted brown rice**
**1 tbs olive oil**
**2 tsp ground cumin seed** (or more to taste)
**Dash black pepper**

Heat in large heavy pan

**2 tbs olive oil**

Flatten bean paste over bottom of pan. Spread rice mixture over bean paste. Make 6 small hollows in rice with back of spoon or whole egg. Break an egg into each hollow. Arrange artistically over rice bed between eggs

**6 thick tomato slices** (or canned tomato halves)
**12 salty black olives***
**6 strips pickled peppers** (optional)

Sprinkle with

**Salt and pepper**
**1 cup grated cheddar cheese**
**Cayenne pepper** (optional)
**Paprika**

Cover tightly. Lower heat. Allow to cook slowly 10 minutes or until eggs are set (soft or firm according to your taste.) Serve to 6 hungry people. If you prefer to bake this, set it in a 300 degrees oven for 20 minutes or until eggs are set.

The several flavours of this dish compliment each other in the most remarkable way.


## TUSCAN BEANS
### Yield: 4 Cups

Heat in heavy pan

**3 tbs oil**

Sauté but do not brown

**¾ tsp chopped garlic**
**¾ tsp sage**

Add

**3 cups cooked drained white beans**
**¾ cup chopped tomato**
**2 tsp red-wine vinegar**
**salt and pepper to taste**

Bring to boil. Reduce heat. Simmer 10 minutes.

---

* The best ones are packed in large tins covered with a brine. Buy them at an Italian or Greek grocery.

# LENTIL LOAF
## Yield: 4-6 Servings

Heat to Boiling

**4 cups water**

Add

**1 cup dry split lentils**

Simmer 30 minutes until tender. Drain. Mash.
Grease a 4 X 9 inch loaf pan.
Heat in heavy pan

**2 tbs oil**

Add and sauté until tender

**1 sliced onion**
**1 diced tomato**
**1 diced apple**
**1 minced clove garlic**

Add to lentils.
Stir in

**1 tsp salt**
**⅛ tsp thyme**
**½ cup milk**
**1 beaten egg**
**1 cup bread crumbs**

Spoon mixture into loaf pan.
Mix

**½ cup bread crumbs**
**1 tbs grated Parmesan cheese**

Sprinkle over loaf. Bake 1 hour in moderate oven.
Serve hot with cheese sauce or cold with yogurt.

# LENTILS AND TOMATOES
## Yield: 4 Cups

A savory Syrian stew.

Add

**1 cup whole washed lentils**

To

**4 cups boiling water**

Return to boil. Simmer 1 hour or until tender. Drain. Reserve
liquid for other use.

Heat in heavy pan

**4 tbs oil**

Add and sauté lightly

**1 chopped green pepper**
**1 chopped onion**
**2 chopped pimentoes**

Add

**2 cups tomatoes**
**½ tsp salt**

Add to lentils

**Dash black pepper**

Simmer 30 minutes uncovered.


## WHITE BEANS AND GREENS
### Yield: 4 Cups

This was my neighbor, Lena's, dandelion recipe. One day we were cutting dandelions under an overgrown hedge when the preacher next door came upon us.

"Oh! excuse me ladies, I didn't see you there."
"We're cutting dandelions."
"Yes, they are a nuisance, aren't they?"

He walked on and we had a good time laughing.

Soak overnight

**1 cup washed white beans**

Cook them in salted seasoned water 2 hours or until tender. Drain. Heat

**1 cup water (or less)**

Add

**1 lb raw or 12 oz frozen greens** (Spinach, kale, dandelions,* etc)

Simmer until tender. Drain.
Heat in a heavy pot

**2 tbs vegetable oil**

Add

**1 clove mined garlic**
**½ inch piece whole dry red chili**

Sauté until garlic begins to brown. Add beans and spinach. Toss together until hot. Serve immediately.

---

* If wild greens are used you may have to blanch (boil briefly) them in lots of water once or twice to get rid of the bitter taste.

# BAKED BEANS
## Yield: 6 Servings

This is the real Boston Bean. The soda is to soften the bean skin without making the whole thing mushy. Rinse them well after blanching. In the 10 minutes blanching with soda, the cooking liquid doesn't have time to penetrate far into the raw bean. Vitamin B destruction should be minimal. The molasses neutralizes any traces of soda left after rinsing the beans. I like to put some Boston brown bread (page 65) into the oven along with the beans for a double treat at supper.

Soak over night

**8 cups water**
**2 cups small white beans**

Next day set oven at 275 Degrees F.
Bring beans and soaking water to boil a large pot.
Add

**½ tsp baking soda**

Boil 10 minutes. Drain. Rinse very well with fresh water.
In the bottom of a bean pot place

**1 onion**
**2 tbs bacon bits** (real or soy product)

Cover with beans
Mix for sauce

**1 tsp dry mustard**
**2 tsp salt**
**Dash black pepper**
**3-4 tbs molasses** (Barbados molasses is perfect)
**A little hot water**

Pour over beans.
Add

**Hot water to just cover**

Cover and bake 4 hours or until beans are tender. When water boils down below the top beans, add just enough to cover them. This is important. The beans should not be allowed to dry out; nor should they be flooded with water.

*Variation* – Rum Baked Beans. Change the sauce to

**1 tsp dry mustard**
**1½ tsp salt**
**dash black pepper**
**1 tbs molasses**
**2 tbs honey**

**3 tbs catsup**
**3 tbs good rum** (light or dark according to your taste)
**2 tbs soy sauce**
**a little hot water**

Continue as above. The result is a lovely, mild flavoured bean. For extra authority stir into the pot of beans just before serving

**2 tbs rum**


## CHILI BEAN PASTE
### Yield: Approximately 1½ Cups paste

Good between slices of bread or rolled up in hot or cold pancakes. Also good in rice and cornmeal dishes or as a side dish in a meal. An excellent traveller. A welcome relief from peanut butter.

Heat in heavy pan

**3 tbs oil**

Sauté 2-3 minutes. Do not scorch!

**1 minced clove garlic**
**½ inch piece whole dry red chili**
**½-1 tsp chili powder** or **½ tsp ground cumin**

Add

**2 cups cooked mashed red beans.**

Sauté and mix. For a finer paste remove hulls by forcing mashed beans through a sieve. Store in covered container in refrigerator.

For variation add 1 tbs bacon bits or onion flakes instead of, or in addition to the chili powder.


## SWEET BEAN PASTE
### Yield: 2½ Cups

The Japanese call it An. The Chinese hide it in the middle of 7 jewel pudding. Try it between slices of bread or rolled up in pancakes or sprinkle it with cinnamon and spread it on hot toast.

Mix

**2 cups mashed cooked red beans**
**3 tbs vegetable oil**
**½ cup sugar**

Store in covered container in refrigerator. For a finer paste remove hulls by forcing bean paste through a sieve. For best success in mashing beans, drain soft cooked beans and mash immediately while steaming hot. Use a wooden or wire potato masher.

# HOW TO SPROUT YOUR OWN BEANS

Wash and pick over

**½ cup mung or soy beans**

Place in a very clean quart jar (dishwasher clean or scalded)
Add

**1 cup tepid water**

Cover loosely.

Set in dark cupboard for 12 hours. Drain. Rinse with tepid water. Drain. Cover loosely. Set jar on its side in dark cupboard. Repeat rinsing and draining and setting on side in cupboard every 12 hours until beans are nicely sprouted. Refrigerate and treat as any tender green vegetable. Your sprouts may not be as long as the Chinese grocer can grow. Never mind that. If they are ½ inch long or more they will be crunchy and tasty. Good to eat as a snack or in salads or stir fry* dishes.

## BEAN SPROUT SALAD #1

Place in a large bowl

**1 cup bean sprouts**
**2 cups cabbage cut in bite-size pieces**
**1 shredded carrot**

Toss lightly with

**French dressing** or **Tangy Dressing** (page 113.)

## BEAN SPROUT SALAD #2

This is not quite like an ordinary salad. The dressing doesn't cling to the bean sprouts. Sprinkle the whole thing over cooked rice or other grain. The flavour is really fine.

Crush in 1 quart bowl

**1 garlic clove**

Add

**¼ cup oil**
**2 tbs vinegar**
**2 tbs soy sauce**
**½ tsp salt**

---

\* To stir fry vegetables, toss them about in a hot oiled pan until just crisp-tender.

**½ tsp pepper**
**2 tbs sesame seeds**

Whip together with a whisk or fork. Remove garlic if you wish.
Add and Toss.

**2 cups bean sprouts**

Toss.

## VEGETABLES

Most cook books, especially traditional ones, have a bounty of good vegetable recipes. It seems that few of them ever get used.

### CAROL'S ONIONS
#### Yield: 4-6 Servings

Set oven at 350 degrees F.

Heat to boiling

**2 cups water**
**1 tsp salt**

Add

**10 small or medium onions**

Heat again to boiling. Simmer 10 minutes. Drain. Place onions in casserole.
Spread over top

**2 tbs ketchup**
**2 tbs water**
**1 tbs butter**
**Dash paprika**

Bake one hour, covered. Remove cover during the last 10 minutes of baking.

### STEWED ONIONS
#### Yield: 1½ Cups

This is Dutch and delicious.

Heat to boiling

**2 cups water**

Add

**3 cups sliced onions**

Simmer until tender. Drain

Melt in small pot

**2 tbs margarine**

Add

**2 tbs flour**

Stir and cook until bubbly.
Slowly add, stirring to blend

**1 cup chicken stock, bouillon or "chicken-in-a-mug"**
**1 tbs lemon juice**

Add onions. Simmer 10 minutes.

## TOMATO POTATOES
### Yield: 3½ Cups

Heat in heavy pan

**2 tbs olive oil**

Sauté until golden

**1 cup finely chopped onion**

Add

**3 cups sliced potatoes**
**1½ tbs tomato paste**
**1 tsp salt**
**Dash pepper**
**Water to barely cover**

Bring to a boil. Reduce heat. Simmer 20 minutes or until potatoes are tender.

# SABZI
## Yield: 2½ Cups

This is Russian and very good.

Heat in heavy pan

**3 tbs margarine**

Add

**¾ cups sliced onions**

Sauté until golden.
Add

**1 chopped large tomato***
**8 shoestring cut carrots**
**½ tsp salt**
**⅛ tsp cayenne pepper**
**Water to barely cover**

Simmer 15 minutes or until carrots are tender and sauce has thickened a bit. Transfer to a heated serving bowl.
Sprinkle with

**¼ cup finely chopped green onions**
**2 tbs finely chopped fresh coriander or parsley**

# FLORENTINE BEANS
## Yield: 3 Cups

Heat in heavy pan

**2 tbs olive oil**

Sauté until golden

**½ minced clove garlic**
**1 tbs sesame seeds**
**½ cup slivered almonds**

Add

**2½ cups cooked salted green beans**

Toss. Heat through. Serve immediately.

For variation substitute 1 cup cooked white beans for 1 cup green beans. If you object to biting the tiny pieces of garlic, omit the minced garlic and sprinkle a bit of powdered garlic on the beans before tossing.

---

* Do you want to do a little extra work and prepare this as the Russians would? Cut the top off the peeled tomato exposing the seed chambers. Gently squeeze the seeds into a sieve. Press them to extract juice from any pulp clinging to them. Save them to plant or to toast and garnish something with. Sauté the tomato over medium high heat until the liquid is evaporated. Then add remaining ingredients and continue as above.

# CABBAGE AND ALMONDS

Heat in heavy pan

**3 tbs oil**

Sauté

**¼ cup slivered almonds***

Remove almonds and set aside.
Add

**1 lb chopped cabbage**
**½ tsp salt**

Stir fry 1 minute. Lower heat. Cover pan. Steam, stirring frequently for 3 minutes or until cabbage is just crisp-tender. Add almonds. Toss. Serve with soy sauce and steamed rice or other grain.

## CABBAGE MORNAY
### Yield: 4 Generous Servings

Set oven at 350 degrees.
Place in a saucepan

**5 cups coarsely shredded cabbage**
**boiling water to cover**

Cover pan. Return to boil. Reduce heat slightly. Boil 2 minutes. Drain, reserving liquid for other use.
Season 1½ cups medium white sauce (recipe page 95) with

**dash cayenne**
**½ cup coarse grated sharp cheddar cheese** (optional)

Add the cooked cabbage, mix, and place in a baking dish.
Butter

**2 slices bread**

Cut into small cubes. Sprinkle over casserole. Bake 30 minutes or until bread is toasted and sauce is bubbling.

## MANITOBA TURNIPS
### Yield: 6 Large Servings

This is the country way to cook turnips in Manitoba. Very satisfying.

Heat to boiling

**4 cups water**
**1 pinch to 1 tsp salt**

---

* For best results with almonds, sauté only the larger uniform pieces leaving the tiny particles for another use as they will burn before the bigger pieces brown.

Add

**6 cups diced turnip**

Cook 15 minutes or until tender. Drain. Mash.
Add

**2 tbs margarine**
**2 tbs brown sugar**
**Salt and pepper to taste**

Beat until fluffy. Serve immediately or keep hot in 250 degrees F. oven.

## CHEDDAR TURNIPS
### Yield: 3 Cups

Heat to boiling

**4 cups water**

Add

**4 cups diced turnips**
**1½ cups diced potatoes**
**½ tsp salt**

Simmer 15 minutes or until tender. Drain. Mash well.
Add

**⅔ cup grated Cheddar cheese**
**1½ tbs finely chopped onion**
**Dash black pepper**
**½ tsp sugar**

Beat until fluffy. Serve immediately or keep hot in 250 degrees oven.

## GLAZED CARROTS
### Yield: 4 Servings

Heat to boiling in medium size pot

**1 to 2 cups water**

Add

**1 lb baby whole carrots** (Or ordinary carrots cut in discreet size pieces)

Return to boiling. Reduce heat. Simmer 15 minutes or until carrots are tender. Drain. Reserve liquid for other use. Heat in heavy pan

**2 tbs butter or margarine**
**2 tbs sugar**
**2 tbs corn syrup**

Add carrots. Simmer, turning carrots frequently until glazed.

# FANCY CHINESE MIXED VEGETABLES
## Yield: 6 Cups

Be brave and try it. You'll be surprised and pleased with the results.

Cut into pretty shapes

**1 medium rutabaga turnip** (balls)
**1 small carrot** (shoestring strips)
**1 large potato** (simple flowers)
**1 medium cucumber** (scored slices)

Heat to furiously boiling

**8 cups water**

Add turnips to water slowly so that water continues to boil. Wait 2 minutes. Add carrots. Wait 3 minutes. Add potatoes and cucumbers. Wait 2 minutes. (If water stops boiling allow extra time.) Drain vegetables carefully so that none are broken. Run cold water over them to cool them. Keep cool in covered container until ready to complete dish.

Heat in wok or heavy pan

**5 tbs peanut oil**
**1 slice ginger**

Sauté above vegetables and

**soaked Chinese mushrooms sliced in half** (soak at least 1 hour before using)

Add

    **2 cups chicken stock**
    **½ tsp salt**
    **½ tsp sugar**

Bring to a boil.
Add

    **⅔ cup cooked macaroni**
    **1 diced bean curd\*** (Optional)

Mix and add to thicken

    **2 tbs corn starch**
    **2 tbs cold water**

## PRAIRIE PINEAPPLE AND SHRIMP
### Yield: 6 servings

Heat to a furious boil in large pot

    **4 cups water**

Gradually add

    **4 oz peeled raw shrimp (or scallops)**

Cook 3 minutes. Remove from boiling water. Splash on cold water. Cut in small pieces. Chill in refrigerator in covered container.

Gradually add to the shrimp water

    **Balls or wedges cut from 1 large turnip (about 2 lb)**

Cook 10 minutes. Drain and reserve liquid. Splash on cold water. Chill in refrigerator in covered container.

Make a paste of

    **1 tbs cornstarch**
    **1 tbs cold water**

Heat in large heavy pan

    **4 tbs oil** (peanut if available)
    **1 slice fresh ginger**

Add and stir fry the shrimps then the turnips.
Add

    **1 tbs medium dry wine**
    **1½ cups soup stock (preferably chicken stock)**

Bring to boil. Reduce heat. Simmer 1 minute. Add cornstarch paste. Return to boil. Sprinkle with

    **1 tbs hot chicken grease** (or oil)

---

\* Get bean curd at a Chinese grocery.

Remove shrimp and turnips to a pretty dish. Pour sauce into a pitcher or boat. Serve with soy sauce and brown rice or other steamed grain. If you were successful in your timing, the turnips will be just crisp-tender and will have a beautiful delicate flavour.

I found these recipes in a book loaned to me by a Chinese student. It was sent to her by her sister in Taiwan. The author studied cooking under the old master Chinese chefs before the Communist take-over of China. She has planned menus for the Red army and she has taught cooking school on TV in Taiwan.

## CAESAR SALAD
### Yield: 6 Servings

Cheap. Nourishing. Far out delicious.
Cut in half

**1 large clove garlic**

Rub a salad bowl with cut surfaces.
Heat in heavy pan

**3 tbs margarine**
**1½ tbs oil**

Add garlic and sauté one minute.
Add

**2 cups cubed day old whole wheat bread**

Sauté until browned. Remove from heat. Pick out garlic and reserve for another use.
Remove leaves from

**1 small cabbage**

Tear into bite-size pieces and place in salad bowl. Reserve ribs and core for another use.
Mix lightly with fork or small whisk

**6 tbs oil**
**3 tbs lemon juice**
**¼ tsp salt**
**Dash pepper**
**1 large egg**

When ready to serve, sprinkle on cabbage, along with

**⅓ cup grated parmesan cheese**
**1 tbs crisp bacon bits** (natural or soy product)

Add croutons and dressing. Toss dramatically and serve.

# GREEK SALAD

Arrange attractively on small plates

> **Shredded cabbage**
> **Small slice feta cheese**
> **2 salty ripe olives**
> **2 quarters boiled egg**
> **Drizzle olive oil over all**

The little bits of things can be varied. Use lettuce, chinese cabbage, bean sprouts, tomato wedges, green pepper rings, sweet onion rings when you have them.

# TANGY SALAD DRESSING
## Yield: 2 Cups

Mix in top of double boiler

> **3 tbs flour**
> **3 tbs sugar**
> **1 tsp salt**
> **1 tsp dry mustard**

Add

> **2 tbs oil**
> **4 well beaten egg yolks** (or **2 whole eggs**)
> **1/3 cup vinegar**
> **1¼ cups water**

Stir constantly over rapidly boiling water 6 minutes or until mixture begins to thicken. Reduce heat and continue to cook and stir 5 minutes more. Pour into bowl or jar. Cover. Cool. Store in refrigerator.

# DESSERTS

We don't eat many desserts – cake on birthdays, pie when we have pumpkin, cookies if Sunshine makes them on Saturday. Dessert lends a festive air, makes a party of a meal.

One summer we were taking our leave of Granny in Parham, Ontario. Luggage and lunch had been packed against the long trip to Winnipeg. We had only to call children for trips to the little house and line up for kisses. Granny eased up to me with a bag of chocolates.

"For the car," she said. "The children will enjoy them."

"Not candy, Mom," I said with obvious hysteria. "It rots their teeth, takes away their appetite for nourishing food, and if they eat too much they get carsick." Granny stopped in her tracks – silent for a minute. "There's boredom," she said and tucked the bag into our car lunch.

So for your parties and to guard against boredom, here are a few recipes for sweet stuff.

You may find some of the recipes too sweet. If so, decrease the amount of sugar. As you become more aware of flavours, an excess of sugar will offend you.

# PLAIN PASTRY
## Yield: 1 – 9 inch Piecrust

There are dozens of pastry recipes. Get one that suits you and make it every day for 5 days. After that you should be able to whip up a pie crust without batting an eye. Here is an old standby that works well.

Set oven at 450 degrees F.
Measure into a bowl and mix

**1 cup flour**
**½ tsp salt**

Rub in or cut in

**¼ to ⅓ cup lard, butter, or shortening**

I like to rub the flour and fat between my fingers until I get a uniform mix. Do this quickly so that the mixture doesn't heat up and the fat become oily.

Quickly sprinkle on drop by drop tossing the dough all the while with the other hand

**2 tbs cold water**

(Use a bit more if you have to, but with practice this small amount does the trick.) Gather the dough into a flattened ball. Flatten it and press it a bit more with the hands. Try not to let the edges crack. Set the dough on a floured board and roll using quick motions with a floured rolling pin. If the dough begins to catch, lift it up off the board and quickly scatter a bit of flour under it. If it catches on the rolling pin, rub a little flour on the rolling pin. Work with a quick light touch. When the circle of rolled pastry is a little bigger than the 9 inch pie pan, (turn the pan over on top of the pastry to measure if you like), fold it in half. Lift it into the corners. Don't stretch it. If the crust has torn moisten the torn edge with a little water, overlap the other edge of the tear and press together. If you have a bare spot on one edge of the pan and excess pastry on the other, moisten the short edge, take a piece of the excess and press into place. Trim off the excess pastry all round and crimp the edges with a finger and thumb or with a fork. If the pieshell is to be baked before filling, prick it slightly with a fork at 3 inch intervals. Bake the pieshell for 10 minutes or until lightly browned. If the pie is to be filled before baking, lower heat to 350 degrees after 10 minutes and continue baking until filling is done.

What about the shortening? A beginner should use the smaller amount. As you gain dexterity in handling piecrust work up to the larger amount if you like a very short crust. I personally prefer a crispy crust to a very short crust so I stick to ¼ cup.

Whole wheat flour works fine in this recipe if you work fast. Bake it at 425 degrees F. instead of 450 degrees F.


## ORANGE CHIFFON PIE
### Yield: 1-9 inch Pie

Try this when you want an out of this world nothing to present to someone. Creamy and good and not too sweet.

Set oven at 400 degrees F.
Mix in top of double boiler in order given

> **3 tbs flour**
> **⅓ cup sugar**
> **Pinch salt**
> **3 egg yolks**
> **2 tbs lemon juice**
> **1 cup orange juice**

Cook and stir over boiling water until very thick. Remove from heat.
Stir in

> **½ tsp vanilla**
> **1 tbs butter or margarine**
> **3 tbs cream or evaporated milk**

Cover pan and set in cold water.
Beat until stiff

> **3 egg whites**

Fold into orange mixture.
Pour into

> **Baked 9 inch pie shell**

Garnish with

> **Sesame seeds**

Bake 10 Minutes. Cool.

## PUMPKIN PIE
### Yield: 1-9 inch Pie

I began to enjoy making pumpkin pie when I found out that I could make it to suit myself instead of to suit a recipe.

Set oven at 450 Degrees F.
Mix

**2 eggs**
**⅓ cup sugar**
**1 cup milk**
**1 cup cooked mashed pumpkin**
**1 pinch salt**
**Seasoning**

Pour into unbaked 9 inch pie shell. Bake 10 minutes. Reset oven to 350 degrees F. Continue to bake 40 minutes or until pie has set and inserted toothpick or knife comes out clean.

Molasses or honey can be substituted for part of the sugar. Light cream or evaporated milk can be substituted for part or all of the milk. Turnip or squash or sweet potato or carrot can be substituted for part or all of the pumpkin.

Seasoning should be to taste. Here is one mixture that I like.

**1 tsp fresh grated ginger**
**½ tsp ground cinnamon**
**¼ tsp ground cloves**
**½ tsp vanilla**

## CHEESE 'N YOGURT PIE
### Yield: 1-9 inch Pie

A pie with a heavenly flavour.

Line

**1 baked 8 or 9 inch pie shell**

With

**1½ cups fresh berries or sliced bananas or thickened fruit sauce**

Sprinkle with

**Small amount of sugar**

Whip or cream together

**½ pound very dry cottage cheese**
**1 cup yogurt**
**1 tbs honey**
**1 tsp vanilla**

116

Spoon over fruit. Chill 4 hours or until well set. Garnish with

**Pieces of fruit or nuts**

I have had the problem of this pie not firming up as it should. It is too lovely a taste though not to pass it along. A teaspoon of gelatin whipped into the yogurt and cheese mixture would help, but I hate to complicate such a simple recipe.

## APPLE CRISP
### Yield: 8 Servings

Always a favourite. A good dish to make for 2 people or 20.

Set oven at 350 degrees F.
Butter 8 by 12 inch baking dish.
Mix

**1 cup flour**
**1 cup rolled oats**
**½ cup brown sugar**
**1 tsp cinnamon**

Cut in or rub in

**½ cup margarine**

Mix with ½ the oat-flour mixture

**4 cups sliced apples**

Spread in baking dish.
Top with remaining oat-flour mixture. Bake 30-40 minutes or until apples are tender and topping is brown.

NOTE – For variation decrease cinnamon to ½ tsp, add 1 tbs lemon juice or ½ tsp of vanilla or both to the apples.

## MATRIMONY SQUARES
### Yield: 24 Squares

A real Canadian cookie. Will marriage remain as an institution? An academic question. But Heaven preserve us if extinction befalls the Matrimony Square.

Set oven at 375 degrees F.
Mix in large bowl

**1 ⅓ cups flour**
**¼ tsp baking soda**
**1¾ cup rolled oats**
**1 cup brown sugar**

Rub or cut in

**¾ cup margarine**

Pat ½ mixture into 9 x 13 inch pan.
Mix in saucepan

**2 cups chopped dates**
**¼ cup sugar**
**1 tbs lemon juice**
**1 cup boiling water**

Simmer gently until soft. Stir to prevent sticking. Cool.

Spread date mixture over oat mixture. Top with remaining oat mixture. Pat gently. Bake until golden (approximately 45 minutes.) Cool. Cut into squares.

## OATMEAL SESAME SEED COOKIES
### Yield: 4 Dozen Cookies

Set oven at 375 degrees F.
Cream until fluffy

**½ cup fat** (butter, lard, margarine, shortening, or a mixture)
**1 cup packed brown sugar**

Add

**1 slightly beaten egg**
**3 tbs milk**

Beat until light and fluffy.
Mix in a separate bowl

**1¼ cup flour**
**1¼ cup small flake rolled oats**
**¾ cups sesame seeds**
**½ tsp salt**
**½ tsp baking soda**
**½ tsp cinnamon**

Add to creamed mixture. Mix well. Drop by rounded teaspoon on ungreased cookie sheet. Flatten slightly with hand or back of spoon. Bake 10 minutes or until brown. Cool on wire racks.

## WHOLE WHEAT CAKE
### Yield: 8 Servings

A light and fluffy cake – tasty too.

Set oven at 350 degrees F.
Grease 8 inch square cake pan. Dust with flour or line with waxed paper.
Cream in large bowl

**¼ cup shortening**

Add gradually

**¾ cups sugar**

Beat until light and fluffy.
Add gradually

**2 beaten eggs**
**½ tsp vanilla**

Beat well. Sift together

**1½ cups whole wheat flour**
**½ tsp salt**
**2 tsp baking powder**

Add to creamed mixture alternately with

**⅔ cups milk**

Mix after each addition, but do not beat. Pour batter into pan. Bake 45-50 minutes until cake springs back to light touch in center or inserted tooth pick comes out clean. Cool 10 minutes in pan, then remove and cool on a wire rack.

*Variations*

1. Cake Flour – Substitute ¾ cup sifted cake and pastry flour for ¾ cup of the whole wheat flour. Makes a very tender cake which almost melts in your mouth. (This is no joke; it really does.)

2. Raisins – Fold **½ cup raisins** into the batter.

3. Topping – Combine

**3 tbs melted margarine**
**5 tbs brown sugar**
**2 tbs light cream, evaporated milk or yogurt**
**1 cup coconut or slivered almonds**

Spread on warm cake. Broil until topping is lightly browned. Warning! Don't leave the oven. This topping browns in 2 or 3 minutes, burns shortly thereafter.

## GINGERBREAD
### Yield: 8 Servings

Quick and tasty.

Set oven at 325 degrees F.
Grease and flour lightly a 9 by 12 inch pan.

Sift together or mix carefully

**1¼ cups whole wheat flour**
**1 cup rye flour**
**⅓ cup sugar**
**1 tsp baking soda**
**1 tsp ground ginger**
**1 tsp ground cinnamon**
**½ tsp salt**

In a separate bowl, mix

**½ cup shortening**
**¾ cup boiling water**
**1 cup molasses**
**1 egg**

Add to dry ingredients and mix. Pour into greased pan and bake 1 hour or until tooth pick comes out clean. Serve warm or cold. Good topped with lemon sauce.

For really great gingerbread, substitute 2 tsp grated fresh ginger for the 1 tsp powdered ginger.

## SWEET LEMON SAUCE

Mix in small pan

**½ cup sugar**
**3 tbs flour**
**1 tsp grated lemon rind**
**¼ tsp salt**

Add gradually, stirring

**1¼ cups boiling water**

Cook over medium heat stirring constantly until thick.
Add

**3 tbs lemon juice**
**2 tbs margarine**

Serve hot on cake or pudding.

## TREACLE STEAKS
### Yield: 6 Steaks

One of those sweet English things from my friend Hope Lee. For tea or bedtime snack.

Mix in small bowl

**1 cup milk**
**1 slightly beaten egg**

120

Dip to coat both sides

**6 – 1 inch slices of whole wheat bread**

Melt and mix in heavy pan

**6 tbs butter or margarine**
**4 tbs sugar**
**6 tbs syrup**

Cook until slightly brown. Add bread. Brown on both sides. Remove to buttered dish and keep hot. Pour over any remaining Treacle. Serve plain or with yogurt.


## CHOCOLATE SYRUP
### Yield: 2 Cups

Mix in saucepan

**1 cup rich dark cocoa**
**1½ cups sugar**
**½ tsp salt**
**1½ cups water**

Bring to a boil stirring until sugar is dissolved. Reduce heat. Simmer 5 minutes. Store in jar with a good lid in a cool place.


## BANANA POPSICLES
### Yield: 6 Popsicles

Mix

**½ cup sugar**
**Dash salt**
**1 egg yolk**
**2 tsp lemon juice**
**½ cup mashed bananas**

Fold in

**2 cups yogurt**

Pour into popsicle molds. Freeze until firm. Very refreshing on a hot day. For variation use crushed pineapple, grated apple, berries or ¼ cup frozen orange juice instead of the mashed bananas.

My daughters, Rain & Sunshine, make popsicles out of any kind of fruit juice. They pour the juice into a plastic glass and put in a spoon (working end down) for a handle.

## CHINESE CHEWS
### Yield: 32 Chews

Especially good keepers, good travellers.

Set oven to 350 degrees F.
Grease 8 inch square pan.
Sift together

> **¾ cup flour**
> **½ cup sugar**
> **1 tsp baking powder**
> **¼ tsp salt**

Add and mix

> **1 cup chopped dates**
> **¾ cup chopped walnuts**
> **2 beaten eggs**

Spread into pan. Bake 30 minutes or until done. Cool slightly. Cut into fingers. Form into balls. Roll in icing sugar. Cool. Store in tightly covered container.

## BREAKFAST FOODS

Recipes for tasty breakfast treats are numerous these days. Here are some that we enjoy.

## YUMMY CRUNCHY GRANOLA
### Yield: 3½ pounds

Make three weeks supply for ever-ready breakfast with milk or yogurt. Good on ice cream or in crumb topping or as the "crispy cereal" in recipes for cookies and squares.

Heat oven to 300 degrees F.
Mix in large bowl

> **8 cups large flake rolled oats**
> **½ cup sunflower seeds**
> **½ cup sesame seeds**
> **1 cup chopped walnuts**
> **1 cup unsweetened coconut**

Melt and mix in saucepan

> **1 cup margarine**
> **1 cup honey**
> **2 tbs milk**
> **1 tsp salt**

Pour over oat mixture. Mix. Spread on two cookie sheets. Bake approximately one hour stirring every 10 minutes then every 5 minutes. Be very careful not to burn on bottom or to overbrown. When about half done stir in

**2 cups raw wheat germ**

Allow to cool on cookie sheets. Store in covered container. Other seeds and nuts may be added or substituted for the ones mentioned.

# SWITZERLAND MUESLI
### Yield: 10½ Cups

Once you get over the initial shock of eating uncooked porridge, you may become a real fan. Muesli is a wonderful food – nearly instant, very nourishing, delicious, versatile and cheap-cheap. A clean taste – truly satisfying.

**#1** Mix and store until needed

**8 cups small flake rolled oats**
**1½ cups raisins**
**1 cup toasted sunflower seeds or other nuts**

Measure out one bowlful for now. Store the rest in covered container.
Grate over bowlful of oats

**½ apple, skin and all**

Melt, mix, and pour over oats and apple

**1-2 tbs honey**
**1 tbs butter or margarine**
**⅓ cup milk**

Mix slightly.

The first time I sat thoughtfully chewing this muesli, I imagined myself the Alm Uncle of Heidi, having breakfast sitting on a little bench outside the chalet high up on my mountainside.

**#2** Measure desired amount of basic oat mixture into cereal bowl

Add

**Chunks of fruit**
**Yogurt**
**Liquid honey**

Mix lightly.

Find a good spot where you can watch the sun coming up. Make yourself comfortable and enjoy your lovely muesli.

**#3** Instant Muesli

To the rolled oat mixture add

>1⅓ **cups Instant skimmed milk powder** (or 1 cup non instant)
>¼ **cup brown sugar**
>½ **tsp salt**

When ready to eat, add

>**Chunks of fruit** (if available)
>**Boiling water**

Mix.

Very handy for back packing trips.


# BARLEY AND RAISINS
## Yield: 5 Cups

In Greece sweetened boiled barley called Iyok is eaten on the feast day of St. Barbara. Season with rose water and lemon for a middle eastern flavour.

Simmer 45 minutes or until tender

>**1 cup pot barley**
>**4 cups water**

Add

>**1 cup raisins**
>**½ cup sugar**
>**1 tsp anise seeds** or **1 tbs lemon juice** and **5 drops rose water.**

Stir. Return to boil. Reduce heat. Simmer 10 minutes.
Garnish with

>**chopped nuts**


# PETER'S PORRIDGE

Try this – it is a unique and satisfying food – an especially good mixture for a vegetarian diet because the proteins of the 3 ingredients are mutually supplementary; the amino acids in scant supply in one food are in more generous supply in another.

Heat to boiling

>**2½ cups water**
>**½ tsp salt**

Add

>**1 cup brown rice**
>**½ cup raw sunflower seeds**
>**½ cup washed soy beans**

Cover pot tightly. Return to boil. Reduce heat. Simmer 45 minutes. May be eaten hot or cold, as is or with milk and fruit. The soy beans remain crunchy and nutlike. On a recent convention and business trip Jerry and I spent 10 days eating mostly on airplanes and in public places. It was Peter's Bean Porridge that I craved.

*Note*: If you don't have sunflower seeds, try unsweetened coconut.

## FERMENTED MILK PRODUCTS

Home yogurt and cheese making should become as popular as home wine making. It is fun to do and oh those delicious results!

### YOGURT
#### Yield: Approximately 4 (32 oz) quarts

Yogurt is a gel made when certain acid forming bacteria are encouraged to grow in sterile milk. Yogurt is a beautiful food with a clean taste. It leaves your tummy feeling so cozy. All you have to do to make yogurt is to introduce some yogurt culture into sterile milk and keep it warm enough for the bacteria to grow. Some people make it in the oven with the light turned on. (If your oven isn't warm enough with the light turned on, you can get a larger wattage bulb for extra heat.) Some people make it in a styrofoam picnic box with a heating pad in the bottom. I met an old lady in a nursing home who made her yogurt in a quart jar wrapped in a blanket in the middle of her bed. It was the only place she had to call her own and it worked fine. Some people buy yogurt makers. Find a method that works well for you.

Here is a good recipe that produces a thick creamy yogurt and here is the method I prefer.

Scald with boiling water

    **6 quart bowl or pot**
    **Measuring cup**
    **Spoon or whisk**
    **3 – 40 oz jars** (or more smaller ones)
    **Lids for jars**

Fill a large pot (must hold the jars you've chosen) with water 120 degrees F. (the temperature of hot dish water)

Put in a grate or something to hold jars off bottom of pot.

Measure into bowl or pot

**10 cups water** (135 degrees F.)
**6 cups instant skim milk powder** (or 5 cups non-instant)
**3 cups evaporated milk**
**1 cup yogurt**

The temperature should be cooled off to 120 degrees F. by the time you add the yogurt. Stir with spoon or whisk until mixed and free from lumps. Pour into jars. Screw on lids. Set in hot water bath. Water should come within 1 inch of tops of jars. If the temperature of the water bath has cooled off, warm it a bit by adding some boiling water or by turning on a little heat under the kettle. Cover the kettle. After 2 hours check the temperature of the water bath. If it has cooled to below 110 degrees F. turn on the heat under the kettle for a few minutes being careful not to raise it above 120 degrees F. After 3 hours begin checking the yogurt every half hour. Tip a jar to one side to see if a firm gel has been formed. This method usually requires 4 hours. When the yogurt has set, chill it immediately. If you don't want to set the hot jars in your refrigerator, fill the sink with cold water to cool them.

If you prefer an overnight method, follow the above recipe but with cooler (120 degrees) water. At bed time set the jars in your electric oven with the light turned on. By morning you should have nicely set yogurt. (My oven stays between 90 and 100 degrees with the light on.)

## POT CHEESE
### Yield: 1 Cup Cheese

This is a very tasty and versatile cheese spread. Use it for sandwiches, to stuff celery stalks or green pepper wedges. Toss a generous spoonful into your macaroni and cheese. Roll balls of it in chopped nuts for salads.

In the middle east it is called Laban and is stored in olive oil until used.

Pour into cloth bag

**4 cups yogurt**

Hang up to drain over night. (Tie it to the tap in the sink or tie to a cupboard door handle and let hang over a bowl. Remove from bag and

**Salt to taste**

If the taste is too sour add

**1 tsp sugar or honey**

Other flavourings such as pimiento, minced onion, bacon bits, nuts may be added at time of use.

126

# COTTAGE CHEESE

The following may seem like a lot of work for a dish of cottage cheese. Try it and you may be pleasantly surprised. The cheese has a beautifully delicate flavour and can be used in many ways. Once you get used to the process, the actual labour involved is very small. You should get about 1⅓ pounds of cheese from 1 pound of skim milk powder.

Scald with boiling water

> **3 quart bowl or pail**
> **Measuring cup**
> **Whisk or slotted spoon**

Measure into pail and mix

> **10 cups warm water** (bath water temperature, 110 degrees F.)
> **4 cups instant skimmed milk powder** (or 3 cups non-instant)
> **1 cup starter***

Incubate at 90 degrees F. constant heat for 11 hours, (any constant heat temperature down to 72 degrees F. should be o.k. but will take longer) or until the milk has set to the consistency of custard. (A sharp knife will leave a clean cut.) If when you check the milk you find that the whey is separated, you will know that it has set too long. A good incubating place in most homes is the kitchen oven with *only* the light turned on. The milk can be set after supper and is ready the next morning.

Cut the Curd. Dip out one cup of curd with a scalded dipper and put it into a scalded container. Stir. Cover tightly. Set in very cold place in back of refrigerator to keep for your next batch of cheese. With a sharp blade that reaches to the bottom of the pail, cut the curd in ¾ inch checkerboard squares. Slash crosswise with the knife to make uniform cubes. Let stand undisturbed 15 minutes.

Cook the Curd. Pour hot water (about as hot as you can tolerate on your hand, 120 degrees F.) over the curds to a depth of 1 inch. Set the pail in a large pot containing water of 120 degrees F. Heat the kettle so gradually that the curd temperature rises 3 degrees every 10 minutes. Very gently rotate the curds, tumbling them over with a spoon, trying not to break them up. Repeat this every 10 minutes. At the end of 1¼ hours the curds should be shrunken quite separate from the whey.

Drain the curd. Dip the curds into a cotton bag or cloth. Reserve the whey for cooking and baking. Wash the curds with tepid then very cold water.

---

* unpasteurized buttermilk or sour cream

Add

**1 tsp salt**

Mix gently. Hang bag up to drain until cheese has reached the consistency you prefer. Store in a covered container in the refrigerator or if the cheese is very dry in the freezer if you wish. If you like creamed cottage cheese, add

**½ cup 20% cream**

Use immediately as is or season with bacon bits, olives, onion or chives or use in salads. Use as a spread or sandwich filling. Good as a side dish especially with spicy bean dishes or curries. Use as filling for fried pies or blintzes or for cheese cake or Cheese'n Yogurt pie (page 116).

*Note*: If possible use low temperature process skimmed milk powder. If there are too many heat damaged protein particles in the milk, the cheese won't make properly.


## BUTTERMILK

Prepare milk for fermentation as directed in the Cottage Cheese recipe. When the curd is set, stir it vigorously with a whisk.
Voilà! Buttermilk. . . .


### Detailed Nutrient and Test Diet Tables

In 1950 in Huntington, West Virginia, Elizabeth Collecta taught Social Studies. Where did you get your information? Will you document that statement? If he says "all" or "none," "always" or "never," he's lying. Make him tell you exactly how many. You deserve to know precisely. I went to college and university a different person because Elizabeth Collecta confirmed my right to demand the facts.

On the following pages are some of the facts on which the assumptions in this book are based. If you wish further verification, I can send you a copy of my research report for the price of xeroxing the 80 pages.

## PERCENTAGE OF TOTAL CALORIES CONTRIBUTED BY MAJOR FOOD GROUPS (1972)

100% = 3,252 Calories

| FOOD GROUPS | FOOD ENERGY |
|---|---|
| Meat, poultry and fish | 20.8% |
| Eggs | 1.7% |
| Milk and Cheese | 11.4% |
| Fats and oils, including butter | 14.7% |
| Fruits | 3.5% |
| Potatoes | 4.4% |
| Vegetables | 1.1% |
| Pulses (legumes) and nuts | 2.5% |
| Flour and cereal products | 20.6% |
| Sugars and other sweeteners | 16.3% |
| Miscellaneous | 3.0% |

SOURCE: *Apparent Per Capita Domestic Disappearance of Food in Canada,* Statistics Canada; Ottawa, 1972.

## NUTRIENTS AVAILABLE FOR CIVILIAN CONSUMPTION PER CAPITA PER DAY

| NUTRIENT | 1971 | 1972 (Preliminary) |
|---|---|---|
| Food Energy (cal.) | 3,320 | 3,300 |
| Protein (gm) | 101 | 101 |
| Fat (gm) | 158 | 156 |
| Carbohydrate (gm) | 381 | 381 |
| Calcium (gm) | .94 | .93 |
| Phosphorus (gm) | 1.54 | 1.53 |
| Iron (mg) | 18.0 | 17.9 |
| Magnesium (mg) | 343 | 341 |
| Vitamin A value (IU) | 8,200 | 8,100 |
| Thiamin (mg) | 1.97 | 1.94 |
| Riboflavin (mg) | 2.37 | 2.36 |
| Niacin (mg) | 23.3 | 23.2 |
| Vitamin $B_6$ (mg) | 2.29 | 2.28 |
| Vitamin $B_{12}$ (mcg) | 9.9 | 9.9 |
| Ascorbic Acid (mg) | 116 | 114 |

Note: Data includes vitamins and minerals added to food products. No deduction is made for wastage in the home.

SOURCE: National Food Situation, November, 1972, USDA, Washington.

## NUTRIENT COMPOSITION OF FOODS ON WEEKLY FOOD LIST

| Food | Weight | Wt. Edible Portion | Calories | Protein | Fat |
|---|---|---|---|---|---|
| Per 100 lb. Stuff | lb | gm | | gm | gm |
| Grains 4 lb. | | | | | |
|   Whole Wheat flour[1] | 2 | – | 3020 | 120.6 | 18.2 |
|   Brown Rice[1] | 2 | – | 3266 | 68.0 | 17.2 |
|   Legumes[2] (White Beans) | .5 | 227 | 760 | 49.5 | 3.6 |
|   SMP | .7 | 317 | 1140 | 114.0 | 2.2 |
|   Fat | .8 | 363 | 3257 | 0 | 360.0 |
|   Sugar | .8 | 368 | 1450 | 0 | 0 |
| Total | | | 12893 | 352.1 | 401.2 |
| Per Person Stuff | | | | | |
|   Eggs – 7 medium | 12 oz | 308[3] | 500 | 39.3 | 35.5 |
|   Cabbage | .6 | 215[4] | 52 | 2.8 | .4 |
|   Carrots | .6 | 240[5] | 101 | 2.6 | .5 |
|   Potatoes | 1.0 | 380[6] | 290 | 8.0 | .4 |
|   Rutabagas | .6 | 240[7] | 106 | 2.5 | .2 |
| Total | | | 1049 | 55.2 | 37.0 |
| Per Adult Stuff | | | | | |
|   Fortified Margarine | .5 | 227 | 1633[8] | 1.4 | 184.0[8] |
| Per Child Stuff | | | | | |
|   Fortified Margarine | .3 | 136 | 980[8] | .8 | 110.1[8] |
|   SMP | .7 | 317 | 1140 | 114.0 | 2.2 |
| Total | | | 1140[8] | 114.8 | 2.2[8] |

[1] Total carbohydrate less fiber rounded to nearest whole number.
[2] Nutrient content of various beans and peas is fairly similar except in soybeans which are a more concentrated source of most nutrients.
[3] Eggs: 11% refuse, shells.
[4] Cabbage: 20% refuse outer leaves and core.
[5] Carrots: 12% refuse, skin.
[6] Potatoes: 16% refuse, skin.
[7] Rutabagas: 15% refuse, skin.
[8] Margarine calories included above in the figure for "Fat" calories – a slightly inflated figure. Margarine is about 80% fat.

| Carbohydrate[1] | Calcium | Iron | Vitamin A Value | Thiamin | Riboflavin | Niacin | Ascorbic Acid (Vitamin C) |
|---|---|---|---|---|---|---|---|
| gm | mg | mg | IU | mg | mg | mg | mg |
| 622 | 372 | 30.0 | 0 | 4.98 | 1.08 | 39.4 | |
| 702 | 290 | 14.6 | 0 | 3.04 | .48 | 42.8 | |
| 126 | 320 | 17.6 | 0 | 1.40 | .49 | 5.3 | |
| 164 | 4100 | 1.9 | 95 | 1.16 | 5.65 | 2.9 | 22 |
| 0 | 0 | 0 | 0 | 0 | 0 | 0 | 0 |
| 368 | 0 | .4 | 0 | 0 | 0 | 0 | 0 |
| 1982 | 5082 | 64.1 | 95 | 10.58 | 7.70 | 90.4 | 22 |
| 3 | 166 | 7.1 | 3645 | .34 | .92 | 3 | 0 |
| 10 | 103 | .9 | 280 | .11 | .11 | .6 | 104 |
| 21 | 89 | 1.7 | 26450 | 1.44 | 1.20 | 1.4 | 19 |
| 63 | 27 | 2.3 | 0 | .38 | .15 | 5.7 | 76[9] |
| 23 | 152 | 1.0 | 134 | .17 | .17 | 2.5 | 99 |
| 120 | 537 | 13.0 | 30509 | 2.44 | 2.55 | 10.5 | 298 |
| 1 | 45 | 0 | 7500[10] | | | | 0 |
| 0 | 27 | 0 | 4500[10] | | | | |
| 164 | 4100 | 1.9 | 95 | 1.16 | 5.65 | 2.9 | 22 |
| 164 | 4127 | 1.9 | 4595 | 1.16 | 5.65 | 2.9 | 22 |

[9] This is an average figure. Values vary from 26 mg/100 gm. for new potatoes to 8 mg/100 gm. for potatoes stored 6 months.

[10] Check your margarine for Vitamin A. Winnipeg margarine would give 800 IU in 5 lb., 4800 IU in 3 lb.

I designed this chart in order to estimate the approximate nutrient intakes of persons planning their meals using the Weekly Food List. I was conservative so that any nutrient furnished in deficient or marginal amounts would plainly show. For a closer estimate, get a food table and figure the values for the specific foods you or your group eats.

See next page for a few examples of persons of different nutrient requirements and their estimated weekly intakes.

## WEEKLY NUTRIENT INTAKES OF PERSONS
## FOLLOWING WEEKLY FOOD LIST

| Sex | Age | Weight in lb | Special Adjustments | Calories | Protein |
|-----|-----|--------------|---------------------|----------|---------|
| M | 30 | 200 | | | gm. |
| Weekly Intake | | | | 26,835 | 759 |
| Canadian Dietary Standard | | | | 28,000 | 380 |
| M | 8 | 50 | | | |
| Weekly Intake | | | | 8,635 | 345 |
| Canadian Dietary Standard | | | | 14,809 | 168 |
| M | 16 | 136 | Figure 175 lb use adult margarine | | |
| Weekly Intake | | | | 24,699 | 789 |
| Canadian Dietary Standard | | | | 25,900 | 325 |
| F | 15 | 108 | Figure 120 lb use adult margarine | | |
| Weekly Intake | | | | 17,689 | 591 |
| Canadian Dietary Standard | | | | 18,200 | 273 |
| F | 30 | 120 | | | |
| Weekly Intake | | | | 16,649 | 477 |
| Canadian Dietary Standard | | | | 16,800 | 273 |
| Nursing Mother | 30 | 125 | Figure 150 lb 1½ x per person stuff per child SMP | | |
| Weekly Intake | | | | 21,920 | 727 |
| Canadian Dietary Standard | | | | 23,800 | 429 |

* There is no official recommendation for daily intake of carbohydrate or fat.

1 You will notice that calorie intake in each case is below Canadian Dietary Standard for the person in question. This is a way of keeping the figures conservative. If protein, mineral and vitamin needs are met before calorie needs, an extra margin of safety is provided.
2 Calculation was done for a person requiring a large amount of calories to check the riboflavin intake.

| Fat | Carbo-hydrate | Calcium | Iron | Vitamin A Value | Thiamin | Riboflavin | Niacin | Ascorbic Acid (Vitamin C) |
|---|---|---|---|---|---|---|---|---|
| gm. | gm. | mg. | mg. | IU | mg. | mg. | mg. | mg. |
| 839 | 4,068 | 10,742 | 141 | 38,199 | 23.3 | 17.8 | 191.3 | 342 |
| * | * | 3,500 | 42 | 25,900 | 8.4 | 14.0 | 84 | 210 |
| 240 | 1,231 | 7,205 | 47 | 35,152 | 8.8 | 11.8 | 58.6 | 331 |
| * | * | 7,000 | 35 | 10,500 | 4.9 | 7.7 | 49.0 | 210 |
| 924 | 3,732 | 13,609 | 127 | 38,270 | 21.9 | 21.5 | 171.4 | 358 |
| * | * | 8,400 | 84 | 22,400 | 7.7 | 13.3 | 77 | 210 |
| 521 | 2,665 | 10,809 | 92 | 38,210 | 16.1 | 17.2 | 121.4 | 346 |
| * | * | 8,400 | 84 | 18,900 | 5.6 | 9.1 | 56 | 210 |
| 518 | 2,468 | 6,682 | 90 | 38,123 | 14.4 | 11.6 | 118.5 | 324 |
| * | * | 3,500 | 70 | 25,900 | 4.9 | 8.4 | 49 | 210 |
| 663 | 3,325 | 12,577 | 118 | 53,737 | 21.3 | 20.8 | 154.7 | 503 |
| * | * | 8,400 | 91 | 36,400 | 7. | 11.9 | 70 | 350 |

# TWO WEEK TEST DIET MENUS (AS EATEN BY 5 PEOPLE)

## WEEK 1

| | BREAKFAST | LUNCH | SNACK | SUPPER |
|---|---|---|---|---|
| Day 1 | Rolled Oat Porridge<br>Wheat Germ & Raisins<br>Toast<br>Margarine<br>Molasses | *Indian Lentil Soup<br>*Brown Bread<br>Margarine<br>Cheese Spread<br>Turnip Sticks<br>Peanut Butter<br>Orange<br>Chocolate Milk | *Granola<br>Raisins<br>Cocoa<br>Hot Lemon | *Minestrone Soup<br>Cole Slaw<br>Green Pepper<br>Italian Dressing<br>*Whole Wheat Bread<br>Margarine<br>*Spaghetti with Tomato Sauce<br>Parmesan Cheese<br>*Apple Crisp |
| Day 2 | Banana<br>*Granola<br>Milk | *Minestrone Soup<br>Peanut Butter<br>sandwich<br>Carrot Sticks<br>Dates<br>Chocolate Milk | *Chinese Chews<br>Hot Lemon | Chicken Noodle Soup<br>*Bean Sprout Salad<br>*Whole Wheat Buns<br>Kasha<br>*Cheddar Turnips<br>Strawberry Ice Cream |
| Day 3 | Pancakes<br>Molasses<br>Oranges<br>Chocolate Milk | *Bread<br>Peanut Butter<br>*Bean Paste<br>Turnip<br>Strawberry Ice Cream<br>*Chinese Chews | Dried Fish<br>(for calcium)<br>Candy | Borscht<br>Carrots Magnifique<br>*Onion Bread<br>*Whole Wheat Bread<br>Syrian Lentils<br>Parsley Potatoes & Peas<br>Lazy Dazy Cake |
| Day 4 | Egg Nogs<br>*Whole Wheat Bread<br>Margarine<br>*Granola | Borscht<br>Peanut Butter/Raisin<br>Sandwich<br>Cheese Spread<br>Carrot Sticks | | *Miso Soup<br>*Fried Cabbage<br>Brown Rice<br>*Bread<br>Vanilla Pudding |

| | BREAKFAST | LUNCH | SNACK | SUPPER |
|---|---|---|---|---|
| Day 5 | Cornmeal Mush<br>*Muesli<br>Milk | *Miso Soup<br>Pancake<br>*Bread<br>*Bean Paste<br>Peanut Butter<br>Honey<br>Cabbage Leaves<br>Carrot<br>*Chinese Chews<br>Vanilla Pudding<br>Apple<br>Chocolate Milk | Cookies<br>Roti<br>Pop | *Chinese Chews<br>Pineapple Juice<br>*Potato Soup<br>*Bean Sprouts<br>*Whole Wheat muffins<br>Mixed Grains (Bulghur Wheat)<br>*Sabzi<br>Orange Chiffon Pudding<br>Jello |
| Day 6 | Red River Cereal<br>Brown Sugar<br>Milk<br>Toasted Muffins<br>Margarine<br>Grapefruit<br>*Bean Sprouts<br>Honey | Carrot<br>*Bread<br>Orange, Apple<br>*Bean Sprouts<br>*Banana Popsicle<br>Cheese Spread<br>Peanut Butter<br>Dried Fish | Potato Chips<br>7-Up | Greek Barley Soup<br>Carrots<br>*Boston Brown Bread<br>*Baked Beans<br>Yogurt Banana Ice Cream<br>Chocolate Milk |
| Day 7 | *Granola<br>*Muesli<br>Margarine<br>Molasses, Maple Syrup<br>*Yogurt Cheese (Pot Cheese)<br>Apple<br>*Whole Wheat Buns<br>Fried Cornmeal Mush | Greek Barley Soup<br>*Onion Bread<br>*Yogurt Cheese Spread<br>Peanut Butter<br>Carrot Sticks<br>Green Pepper<br>Turnip<br>Chocolate Milk<br>*Matrimony Squares | Hot Lemon | *Miso Soup<br>Anti Pasta<br>Puri<br>*Curried Vegetables<br>Brown Rice<br>*Dal<br>*Matrimony Squares<br>Pumpkin Pie<br>Curried Eggs |

| | BREAKFAST | LUNCH | SNACK | SUPPER |
|---|---|---|---|---|
| Day 8 | *Granola<br>Milk | *Potato Soup<br>Milk<br>Peanut Butter or Cheese Sandwich<br>*Matrimony Squares<br>*Pumpkin Pie<br>Carrots, Turnip<br>Green Pepper<br>Muffins | Apple Popsicle<br>Cashews<br>Dried Fish<br>Cookies<br>Sunflower Seeds | *Pea Soup<br>Apple-Cabbage Salad<br>Creamy Dressing<br>*Barley Casserole<br>*Manitoba Turnips<br>Orange Cookies<br>*Rye Bread |
| Day 9 | Grapefruit<br>French Toast | *Pea Soup<br>*Rye Bread<br>*Yogurt Cheese Spread<br>Turnip Sticks, Carrots<br>Peanut Butter<br>Orange Cookies<br>Grapefruit<br>Matrimony Squares | Chocolate<br>Popcorn | Greek Lentil Soup<br>*Chutney<br>Puri<br>*Curried Vegetables<br>Brown Rice<br>*Stewed Onions<br>Gingerbread<br>Custard Sauce |
| Day 10 | Oatmeal Porridge<br>*Granola<br>Milk<br>Toast<br>Margarine | Greek Lentil Soup<br>Peanut Butter/Honey Sandwich<br>Cabbage Leaf, Apple<br>Cheese Spread<br>Gingerbread<br>*Stewed Onions<br>Orange Cookies<br>Milk | Granola<br>Green Pepper<br>Apple | Greek Potato Soup<br>*Bean Salad<br>*Whole Wheat Buns<br>*Cabbage Rolls<br>Turnip Pie |

| | BREAKFAST | LUNCH | SNACK | SUPPER |
|---|---|---|---|---|
| Day 11 | Whole Wheat Pancakes<br>Margarine<br>Honey & Molasses<br>Grapefruit | *Greek Potato Soup<br>Peanut Butter<br>Turnips<br>*Bean Paste<br>*Bread<br>Grapefruit | Grapefruit<br>Chocolate-coconut Candy | *French Onion Soup<br>Cabbage Raisin Pineapple Salad<br>Yogurt Dressing<br>French Bread<br>Steamed Wheat<br>Greek Braised Potatoes<br>Orange Cookies<br>Spice Cake |
| Day 12 | *Barley & Raisins<br>Oatmeal Porridge<br>Toast<br>Margarine, Honey | Greek Lentil Soup<br>*Stewed Onions<br>*Bread<br>Cheese Spread<br>Cheddar Cheese<br>Peanut Butter<br>Carrot Sticks<br>Boiled Onion<br>Pineapple Popsicles<br>Cookies | Toffee<br>Muesli<br>Apple<br>Orange | Orange Onion Salad<br>Corn Pone<br>*Chili Con Frijoles<br>Rice Pudding |
| Day 13 | *Muesli<br>Milk | Noodle Soup<br>Turnips & Peanut Butter<br>*Brown Bread<br>Pineapple Sherbet | Grapefruit<br>Cocoa | *Lasagna<br>Lettuce-Tomato Salad |
| Day 14 | *Muesli | *Whole Wheat Bread<br>*Muesli<br>Margarine<br>Cucumber, Carrots<br>Blue Cheese<br>Orange Juice<br>Pineapple | *Granola<br>Dried Apples | Macaroni & Cheese<br>White Bread<br>Peanut Butter<br>Grapefruit |

**Daily Nutrient Intakes Recommended for Adults and Children**

| Sex | Age Yrs. | Weight Lbs. | Activity Category | Calories | Protein g[1] | Calcium g | Iron mg | Vitamin A IU[2] | Vitamin D IU | Ascorbic Acid mg | Thiamin mg | Riboflavin mg | Niacin mg |
|---|---|---|---|---|---|---|---|---|---|---|---|---|---|
| Both | 1-2 | 20-26 | Usual | 900-1200 | 12-16 | 0.7 | 5 | 1000 | 400 | 20 | 0.4 | 0.6 | 4 |
| Both | 4-6 | 40 | Usual | 1700 | 20 | 0.7 | 5 | 1000 | 400 | 20 | 0.5 | 0.9 | 5 |
| Both | 10-12 | 77 | Usual | 2500 | 30 | 1.2 | 12 | 2000 | 400 | 30 | 0.8 | 1.3 | 8 |
| Boy | 16-17 | 136 | B | 3700 | 45 | 1.2 | 12 | 3200 | 400 | 30 | 1.1 | 1.9 | 11 |
| Girl | 16-17 | 120 | A | 2400 | 41 | 1.2 | 12 | 3200 | 400 | 30 | 0.7 | 1.2 | 7 |
| Woman | | 124 | Maintenance | 1900 | 39 | 0.5 | 10 | 3700 | - | 30 | 0.6 | 1.0 | 6 |
| | | | A | 2400 | 39 | 0.5 | 10 | 3700 | - | 30 | 0.7 | 1.2 | 7 |
| | | | B | 3000 | 39 | 0.5 | 10 | 3700 | - | 30 | 0.9 | 1.5 | 9 |
| | | | C | 3550 | 39 | 0.5 | 10 | 3700 | - | 30 | 1.1 | 1.8 | 11 |
| Man | | 158 | Maintenance | 2300 | 48 | 0.5 | 6 | 3700 | - | 30 | 0.7 | 1.2 | 7 |
| | | | A | 2850 | 48 | 0.5 | 6 | 3700 | - | 30 | 0.9 | 1.4 | 9 |
| | | | B | 3650 | 48 | 0.5 | 6 | 3700 | - | 30 | 1.1 | 1.8 | 11 |
| | | | C | 4250 | 48 | 0.5 | 6 | 3700 | - | 30 | 1.3 | 2.1 | 13 |

[1] Protein recommendation is based on normal mixed Canadian diet. Vegetarian diets may require a higher protein content.

[2] Vitamin A is based on the mixed Canadian diet supplying both Vitamin A and Carotene. As preformed Vitamin A the suggested intake would be about 2/3 of that indicated. Vegetarian diets may require up to 7500 IU.

SOURCE: Canadian Council on Nutrition, "A Dietary Standard for Canada," 1963.

# SOME COOKBOOKS WITH
# GOOD LOW COST RECIPES

1. Arends, Savelkeul, L., Van der Sar-Vuyk; J. M., Senior-Baiz, E, *Cookbook of the Netherland Antilles*, Boekhandel Salas, Curacao, Netherlands Antilles, 1968.
2. *Argenta Cookbook*, Argenta Friends School, Argenta, B.C., 1971.
3. Bennet, Paula Pogamy & Clark, Velma R. *Cooking the Hungarian Way*, Garden City, New York: Doubleday & Co., 1954.
4. Brown, B. & Rose, C. *The Country Cookbook*, New York: A. S. Barnes and Company, 1937.
5. *Canadian Whole Earth Almanac*, Vol. 2, No. 3, Fall, 1971, Healing, Canadian Whole Earth Research Foundation, 341 Bloor St., Toronto.
6. Cass, Elizabeth, *Spanish Cooking*, London: Andre Deutsch Limited, 1957.
7. Corey, Helen, *The Art of Syrian Cookery*, Garden City, New York: Doubleday & Co. 1962.
8. Ekambaram, Manorama, *Hindu Cookery*, Bombay, India: D. B. Taraporevala Sons & Co., 1963.
9. Food Editors of Farm Journal, *Homemade Bread*, Garden City, New York: Doubleday & Co., 1969.
10. Lappé, Frances Moore, *Diet for a Small Planet*, New York: Ballantine Books, 1971.
11. Lin, Hsiangjul & Tsuifeng, *Secrets of Chinese Cooking*, Englewood Cliffs, New York: Prentice-Hall, 1960.
12. Mendelsohn, Oscar A., *A Salute to Onions*, New York: Hawthorne Books Inc., 1965.
13. Pinto, Maria Lo, *The Art of Italian Cooking*, Garden City, New York: Doubleday & Co., 1948.
14. Rombauer, Irma S., Becker & Marion, *Joy of Cooking*, Indianapolis, Ind: Bobbs-Merrill Co., 1964.
15. Smetinoff, Olga, *The Yogurt Cookbook*, New York: Pyramid Books, 1971.
16. *The All New Purity Cook Book*, Winnipeg: Maple Leaf Mills Ltd., 1967; or Box 52, Toronto.
17. *Purity Cook Book*, Western Canada Flour Mills Ltd., Toronto 1936.
18. Thompson, Edna, *Yoga Cookbook*, New York: Philosophical Library, 1959.
19. Time-Life Books, *Recipes: African Cooking*, New York, 1970.
20. Van Limberg, Stirum, *Art of Dutch Cooking*, Garden City, New York: Doubleday & Co., 1961.

21. Weiner, Joan, *Victory Through Vegetables*, New York: Holt, Rinehart & Winston, 1970.
22. Wolcott, Imogene, *The New England Yankee Cookbook*, New York: Coward-McCann Inc., 1939.
23. Women of St. Paul's Greek Orthodox Church, Hempstead, Long Island, N.Y., *The Art of Greek Cookery*, Doubleday & Co., 1963.

## BIBLIOGRAPHY

1. Altschul, A. M., *Proteins: Their Chemistry and Politics*, New York: Basic Books, 1964.
2. Canadian Council on Nutrition, 1963. "Dietary Standard for Canada," pp. 9, 10, 11, Table I, Table II, as excerpted by the Faculty of Home Economics, University of Manitoba, Winnipeg.
3. FAO/WHO Expert Group, 1965. "Protein requirements," *WHO Technical Report*, Series No. 301, WHO, Rome.
4. Rose, W. C., "The Amino Acid Requirements of Adult Man," *Nutr. Abst. Rev.*, 1957, pp. 27, 63.
5. USDA, "Composition of Foods, Raw, Processed, Prepared" (called Handbook #8), Washingtron, 1963.
6. USDA, "National Food Situation," Washington, August, 1972.
7. USDA, "National Food Situation," Washington, November, 1972.

## General Index

**A**

Ascorbic Acid, see vitamin C

**B**

Baking powder, action, 59 – 60
Baking soda action, 59 – 60
Barley, nutrients, 35
Beans, nutrients, 36
Beef liver, net protein utilization, 44
Beef muscle, net protein utilization, 44
Buckwheat, nutrients, 35
Butter
  in test diet, 40
  shortening power, 57

**C**

Cabbage, in test diet, 38 – 39
Calcium, 38, 49
Calories
  sources, 13, 19, 20
  test diet, 29, 43
Candy, 40
Carrots, test diet, 38 – 39
Chemical leavening agents, 59 – 60
Cornmeal, nutrients, 35
Costs of food, 13 – 15, 19 – 20, 32 – 33

**D**

Diet
  for one person, 49 – 51
  planning, 46 – 48
  typical North American, 12, 24
Digestion, 52

**E**

Eggs
  net protein utilization, 44
  test diet, 38, 43, 49
Ever ready foods, 47

**F**

Fat,
  body, 48 – 49
  oils, 40, 43, 56 – 57
Fish, net protein utilization, 44
Flour, 35, 58 – 60
Fruits
  dried, 40, 42, 47
  fresh, 24, 47

**G**

Grains, nutrients, 34 – 35

**H**

Honey, 40, 42, 52, 60

**I**

Iron, 19, 35, 37, 38, 49

**L**

Lard, 56 – 57
Legumes
  nutrients, 36 – 37
  test diet, 43, 44
Lentils, nutrients, 36

**M**

Margarine, test diet, 32, 40
Meat, 10, 13, 19 – 20, 43
Milk
  net protein utilization, 44
  test diet, 31, 37, 43
Millet, 33, 35
Molasses, 40, 42, 60

**N**

Nutrient
  contents, 14, 22, 28, 35, 36, 38, 41, 44
  requirements, 14, 21, 29, 31, 33, 37, 41, 43, 44, 53
Nuts, nutrients, 35, 37

**O**

Oats, nutrients, 35
Oil, vegetable, 56

**P**

Peanut flour, net protein utilization, 44
Peas, 36
Potato
  net protein utilization, 44
  test diet, 37 – 39
Protein
  cost of animal, 13, 14, 19, 20
  quality, 44, 45
  test diet, 37, 38

**Recipe Index**